# Communicating Effectively

## Tools for Educational Leaders

Michael B. Gilbert

SCARECROWEDUCATION
Lanham, Maryland • Toronto • Oxford
2004

Published in the United States of America
by ScarecrowEducation
An imprint of The Rowman & Littlefield Publishing Group, Inc.
4501 Forbes Boulevard, Suite 200, Lanham, Maryland 20706
www.scarecroweducation.com

PO Box 317
Oxford
OX2 9RU, UK

British Library Cataloguing in Publication Information Available

**Library of Congress Cataloging-in-Publication Data**

Gilbert, Michael B., 1944–
    Communicating effectively : tools for educational leaders / Michael B.
Gilbert.
        p.   cm.
    Includes bibliographical references.
    ISBN 1-57886-035-0 (pbk. : alk. paper)
    1. Communication in education–United States.   2. School management
and organization–United States.   I. Title.
    LB1033.5 .G55   2004
    371.102′2–dc21                                      2003014138

∞ ™ The paper used in this publication meets the minimum requirements
of American National Standard for Information Sciences—Permanence of
Paper for Printed Library Materials, ANSI/NISO Z39.48-1992. Manufactured
in the United States of America.

This book is dedicated to my children—Norman, Rhoda, Alexa, and Emma: You are the hope of the future and the models of what I have learned about parenting and people. I love you all very much.

# CONTENTS

Appendices:

# ILLUSTRATIONS

## FIGURES

## TABLES

# FOREWORD

Educational administration/management is the service of leading someone by the hand. That's what Dr. Michael Gilbert does so masterfully in
this book. He walks with the reader, giving a step-by-step lesson plan
for educational managers and leaders in how to connect, motivate, and
resolve conflict throughout their administrative responsibilities. Dr. Gilbert shares the secrets of how to communicate with all types of colleagues, including how to talk each one's language (perception), how to
motivate each one individually (psychological need), and how to resolve
conflicts easily and effectively.

Dr. Gilbert is an educator of educators, and an expert in the Process
Communication Model (PCM). PCM profiles, seminars, and books have
been applied in business, management, sales, teams, mentoring, parenting, health fields, religion, politics, and in education for the past twenty
years, touching the lives of more than a half million people, in dozens
of countries.

With a solid foundation of research (including many dissertations),
the Process Teaching Model (PTM) promises to be one of the most significant contributions to educational leadership. Former President Bill
Clinton publicly acclaimed to his secretary of education that this model
of teaching, learning, and communicating "is a great contribution to education."

I am lucky to have discovered the fabric of processes that holds together the contents of how we communicate. I am fortunate to have
such a friend and colleague as Dr. Michael Gilbert, who has devoted his
life to educating educators.

Michael's examples of real-life problems and solutions, insights into
behaviors, plans for success, and integrations of classic approaches are
as appealing to the seasoned academician as they are to the student

teacher. With respect and pride, I pass the PCM torch to Dr. Michael Gilbert in educational administration/management. With his vast experience, myriad professional accomplishments, and expansive knowledge of all levels of education, Michael, I believe, will help light the way of achieving our PCM/PTM mission: to significantly enhance the quality of lives for generations.

—TAIBI KAHLER

Taibi Kahler is a clinical psychologist and organizational consultant in Little Rock, Arkansas. He is the creator of the Process Communication Model that underpins this book. He is also a close advisor to former President Bill Clinton and Senator Hillary Rodham Clinton, who was the catalyst for my meeting Dr. Kahler and getting to understand and use his work.

—MICHAEL GILBERT

# PREFACE

The field of educational administration/management is replete with books that deal with the technical, conceptual, and human concepts related to programs and personnel in schools and school districts. This book focuses on the critical underpinning of human interaction—communication.

I wrote this book because of two "Ah ha!" experiences I had along my professional way. These profound eye-openers (for me, at least) have made a major difference in both my personal and professional lives.

More than twenty years ago, I encountered the first "Ah ha!" when I was watching television one day. There was what appeared to be a public service announcement sponsored by the Sperry Corporation (now Unisys) suggesting that those at Sperry had learned to listen. That message caught my "ear." Why was this an important thing to say? Don't we all listen?

So I wrote to Sperry, asking for more information about what they were doing with listening. After a protracted period, they sent me a copy of their "Personal Listening Profile," and wished me well. Fortunately, the profile gave credit to its creator, one Dr. Lyman K. Steil of the University of Minnesota.

I wrote to Dr. Steil, who responded by sending me numerous articles on listening and by inviting me to join the fledgling International Listening Association (ILA)—which I did. My affiliation with the ILA has been most rewarding, but puzzling as well. In my many years of membership, I have found I am in a distinct minority of membership status. That is, I have not found any other members who do what I do—assist education professionals preparing to be administrators and leaders.

What this has said to me is two things: (1) quite naturally, educators choose to be a part of organizations that focus broadly on what they do—that is, those that focus on knowledge and skills to administer educational organizations (e.g., the American Association of School Administrators, the Association for Supervision and Curriculum Development, and others), and (2) the emphasis on listening may not be part of what some see those critical knowledge and skills for educational leaders to be. I have found both contentions to be accurate over the years. The overall problem seemed to be that educators were and are inadequately prepared to do what they need to do—communicate effectively with students, parents, and colleagues.

The second "Ah ha!" came more than ten years ago, subsequent to a suggestion from Senator Hillary Rodham Clinton, then first lady of Arkansas. She thought my meeting Dr. Taibi Kahler would be useful because of our mutual professional interests. She was right.

Dr. Kahler, using his background in clinical psychology, had developed a highly comprehensive interaction assessment and training tool he called the "Process Communication Model" (PCM). He was most generous with his time and mentored me in my understanding of PCM. He had applied the model to organizational settings and had worked with numerous companies and agencies—most notably, the National Aeronautics and Space Administration (NASA).

These two events led to my exploration of the concepts as they relate to developing the knowledge and skills needed by educational leaders—hence, this book.

There is a story (or maybe a fable) that periodically circulates through organizations:

It seems that an employee with a problem walks into a meeting with his supervisor. As he enters the meeting and either because the supervisor knows the purpose of the meeting or picks up some nonverbal cues, he says, "I see you've brought your monkey with you." (Of course, he is alluding to the colleague's problem.)

"We will take as much time as we need to talk about your monkey. You can tell me whatever you think I need to know about your monkey. We will examine your monkey up one side and down the other. We will give your monkey whatever attention you think it needs, but when we are finished, knowing that it is *your* monkey, you will take your monkey with you."

We know that people want to avoid conflict. For most, conflict is uncomfortable. When we need to confront the incompatibilities we see between us and others, we would prefer many times that someone else deal with the problem. So we want them to take care of our "monkey." The issue is how to communicate effectively in order to resolve conflict and solve problems. The operative word is *effective*. There are many who can do the job (that is, they are efficient) but fewer who can do the job right (that is, be effective). Maybe this is also the distinction to be made between management and leadership (Bennis and Nanus 1985)—managing conflict or leading people through conflict to resolution.

This book is designed for educational leaders to deal with the communication issues they confront. The concepts come from a variety of fields—communication, organizational theory, and practice—and are blended with suggestions for educational leaders. The underlying notion is that if educators can communicate effectively, it will be easier to implement programs successfully and the attendant problems will be fewer and less intense. The basis of this effective communication is understanding how people prefer to communicate and interact, what motivates them, and what happens when their needs go unmet.

My years in professional education—at the school site, in the school district, and in educator preparation—have provided the base of experience for this book. For your consideration, I have presented:

1. Some ideas based on research,
2. A look at the types of people who are educators,
3. Suggestions for dealing with examples of situations you may encounter, and
4. Suggestions for keeping yourself and those with whom you interact energized.

I have tried to present the gist of the concepts. For those of you who are interested in some of the research particulars, they appear in the appendices.

I agonized over how to write this book. The first part has a decidedly didactic tone, imparting information and ideas with the appropriate support from the field. As I got into more of the Process Communication concepts, my writing relaxed a bit. For those of you who prefer a more casual style, I hope you will forgive the more formal writing. For those of you who prefer the structure of a more academic style, I hope you will savor the relaxed passages.

For all of you, I trust you will enjoy what you read, find value and good ideas in what is presented, be able to reflect on past and future practice, see ways to connect with your coworkers and the significant other people in your life, and set a course for yourself.

Your ability to be an effective leader comes from who you are, how well you can get your own needs met and keep yourself motivated, and your powers of effective listening and observation to assist others. On your journey, you will meet educators who will stimulate you—first by asking you to understand how people behave (and miscommunicate), and then by challenging you to recognize whose problem it is and to find the right person and technique to address it.

You will be introduced to six educators. Each represents a different personality type. The character strengths, interaction styles, perceptions, needs, and patterns of miscommunication described about them are universal (Kahler 1988). They are aspects of personalities you face every day in the world of education (and beyond). If you refine these basic aspects of understanding people with care and learn to identify their subtleties with skill and attention, you will enhance your ability to lead and empower others.

The right tools for educational leadership vary with each "builder" as he or she interacts with others. *Effectiveness* emerges when we understand why people do what they do. Do you know what motivates a person to be successful, to accomplish, and to achieve? And do you know what leads the same person into negative, nonproductive behavior? If your answer is yes, then you hold the key to being an effective educational leader by having the right tools.

This book is adapted from an eclectic but practical body of knowledge that will help you translate the observable behaviors of others into useful and effective patterns of interaction for each person in your work life. (You will find there is also a carryover to your personal life.)

I invite you to examine your leadership, communication, and interaction skills as you discover how to solve the problems in your life. As I have used these concepts in my personal and professional life, I have experienced one of the most dramatic metamorphoses one can imagine.

Those with whom I interact and those who ask me to mentor them have said this information is among the most important and enlightening for them as well. I trust you will find it equally valuable. Perhaps, when you finish reading this book, you, too, may say, "Ah ha!"

## REFERENCES

Bennis, W. and B. Nanus. 1985. *Leaders: The strategies of taking charge*. New York: Harper and Row.

Kahler, T. 1988. *The mastery of management*. Little Rock, Ark.: Kahler Communications.

# Acknowledgments

I am indebted to Taibi Kahler for his generous guidance and mentoring of me in my understanding of his prodigious and comprehensive Process Communication Model, and for his kind comments in the foreword.

I thank Hillary Rodham Clinton for her suggestion that I meet and get to know Dr. Kahler. Her suggestion has made a profound difference in my life.

I am particularly grateful to Ray Bruce for his long-term and unflagging friendship. His unselfish counsel over the years has been gentle and wise . . . and much appreciated.

Those others who have had a significant impact on my professional development include Carroll W. McGuffey and Linton Deck, both of whom have taught me a great deal by word and by example.

I appreciate the introduction to the "world of listening" provided by Manny Steil. I also acknowledge Bob Bolton, whose wisdom and work I admire.

I thank the myriads of educators who have been my students for the honor of working with them and for what they have taught me. I am a better person for having known and worked with all of these people.

# SECTION I

## RAW MATERIALS: LEADERSHIP CONCEPTS

# ONE

## The Beginning Stage

*Leaders* may be defined as goal-directed people who can influence others to follow a path toward that goal. Leaders encourage others to go places they would not go by themselves (Barker 1999). Leaders may be titular—that is, vested with the authority to lead by virtue of their position in an organization—or they may be genuine—able to lead regardless of their organizational status. In effective organizations, titular leaders are also genuine leaders.

Historically, many school administrators embraced an approach to leadership that is quite parental. They viewed the school organization as a quasi family, with all the major decisions made by the family head. This approach disables or disenfranchises the professionals within the organization from important decisions that affect them.

If professional staff are *controlled* because others make decisions for them, it is not unusual to see these staff members adopt a controlling attitude with students. In this type of organization, people are not led; they are pushed.

During his tenure as commander of the Allied forces in World War II, General Dwight Eisenhower used the following analogy to exemplify leadership. He said that if a string is laid on the floor and pushed at one end, not much happens. However, if one pulls the string, a lot more progress is made. Leading can be seen as "pulling the string," *encouraging* others to go in new directions.

Distinguishing between pushing and pulling might compare to bossing and leading. *Bossing* is characterized as telling without asking for input, evaluating without collaborating, and coercing others to perform;

*leading* involves others by seeking their input, looking to them as primary sources of performance evaluation, and trusting coworkers to make appropriate decisions in a collegial way (Glasser 1990).

These characteristics are similar to the Theory X and Theory Y propositions offered by Douglas McGregor (1960). Theory X presumes subordinates need to be controlled and will not work well without stringent oversight. Theory Y presumes subordinates will contribute to the goals of the organization because there is something intrinsically gratifying about doing a good job; these people need minimal oversight.

## COMMUNICATE TO SUCCEED

In many respects, effective leadership is related to your ability to communicate and your willingness to understand issues from another person's perspective. Many people have difficulties in their professional and personal lives because of poorly developed or poorly used communication skills. Simply stated, communication is understanding what another wants to convey. Developing your communication skills is tied inexorably to being an effective leader.

Understanding what people need as individuals is a principal determinant in effective communication. Instructionally, this is embedded in the interaction between teachers and students. A "variety of empirical research has documented significant relationships between personality traits of teachers and their classroom behavior" (Kagan and Grandgenett 1987, 12). The impact of different personality characteristics and needs is important in classroom environments: "Differences in psychological type between teachers and students can lead teachers to misunderstand learning styles of students" (Bargar and Hoover 1984, 59). It is important that teachers understand student personality types and how personality types can affect learning. Their personality types affect how well teachers analyze student needs, how much time they spend on instruction and management, how much time students engage in learning, and the level of student achievement.

It is crucial to match teaching style with learning preference (Gilbert 1996, 1999). This principle may be mitigated by opportunity—that is, teaching staff may not have a full range of teaching styles because of their preferences or their ability to use other strategies.

Other roadblocks may be school organization or size. Many schools are organized into self-contained units, providing little instructional interaction among professional staff in the delivery of curricula.

Schools may also be constrained by size. If an elementary school is *graded* and there is only one teacher per grade, then assigning students to teachers with different styles is moot. The effectiveness of small schools has been debated for some time without conclusive evidence to affirm and refute optimal size (see Gilbert [2000] for a recent examination of the issue).

The extension to how schools and their staffs are administered is not a quantum leap. It is important that those who supervise teaching and other school activities have a full range of decision styles—*telling, selling, participating* (or consulting), and *delegating* (or joining) (Hersey, Blanchard, and Johnson 1996). All are appropriate, and one should not be used exclusively. Choosing which style to use is based on factors in the situation, the leader, and those who participate in various organizational decisions. In effective organizations, those who implement decisions should make them as much as possible. Full use of this strategy depends on the time available to make a decision and the maturity of those who would make those decisions. As with teaching styles, the choice of effective decision styles is based on what people need. The determination of needs and the effective communication used to help people succeed are the focus of this book.

### Audiences to Consider

Educational leaders deal with a number of different audiences, inside and outside of the school organization. Each of these audiences holds a different stake in what the school is about and what it produces. Effective communicators must know how to deal with each audience in ways that satisfy their need to know and to function well.

The various audiences include students, staff (site and central office), parents, and community. Each group needs to know different things. Students need to know the expectations of learning. Staff need to know the building blocks ("whats") and tools and strategies ("hows") of their jobs. Parents want to know how their children are doing (and how they can support the school). Communities (society) want to know how well the students will fit into an overall plan for the future.


## Moving Ahead

The deft shift in communication styles distinguishes a leader from a manager. Effective leaders adjust their style to help others meet their needs.

The greatest benefit of more effective communication is that it spreads throughout the organization—among administrators and staff, staff and students, and staff with each other. Moreover, this benefit carries over into the home, where communication becomes more effective between the individuals and their families.

Many educators subscribe to the notion that students and staff must be structured into specific patterns in order for them to succeed. This narrow view limits people and thwarts their success, in school and beyond. Understanding ourselves and others, knowing what negative behaviors mean and what to do about them in the school setting, and focusing more on *how* we communicate may have profound consequences in education.


## EFFECTIVE EDUCATIONAL LEADERSHIP

Educational leaders confront conflict of one type or another on a fairly regular basis. This conflict may be productive or it may cause varying degrees of unrest and damage to working relationships. Conflict may be personal (within oneself), behavioral (involving interaction), or structural (relationships between different aspects of an organization) (Bondesio 1992). Conflict involves two or more people with incompatible positions or perspectives. Perhaps it is better described as the *perception* of incompatible positions. (As some have said, "Perception is reality.") The management—moreover, the resolution—of conflict is the ongoing test of administrative effectiveness. If one can communicate effectively, one can attempt to resolve most, if not all, conflicts with more tools to change perceptions or to use differing perceptions to arrive at a mutually acceptable resolution.

One may choose from among five strategies or techniques of conflict management (see chapter 10 for a more extensive discussion). The possibilities range from *withdrawal* and *suppression* to *domination, compromise,* and *integration* (or *collaboration*). Whether one ignores conflict or takes a position where dissatisfaction remains, the conflict is likely to resurface. (If the conflict causes the relationship to disintegrate, then the conflict may no longer be an issue because the competing parties do not interact with each other.) The true resolution of conflict involves both parties being satisfied—the *win/win* position. In order to get to that juncture, one must be adept in understanding the position of the other party to the conflict and also be able to assert an alternate position in a palatable manner. To do this requires productive communication. In terms of transactional analysis, the target position would then be "I'm OK—You're OK" (Berne 1964; Ernst 1973; Harris 1969; Harris and Harris 1985).

From the classical, eclectic background literature of management and administration, one of the requisites of organization is that "there are persons able to communicate with each other" (Barnard 1938, 82). Further, communication occupies "a central place, because the structure, extensiveness, and scope of organization are almost entirely determined by communication techniques" (91). Conversely, "the absence of a suitable technique of communication would eliminate the possibility of some purposes as a basis for organization" (90). In sum, "the first executive function is to develop and maintain a system of communication" (226).

When one applies communication psychologically to administrative decisions,

> General organization decisions can control the behavior of the individual only through psychological mechanisms that bring values and knowledge to bear upon each individual decision at the time it is made. . . . Failures in communication result whenever it is forgotten that the behavior of individuals is the tool with which the organization achieves its purpose. (Simon 1957, 107–8)

Channels of communication are not necessarily tied to lines of author- ity. Functional communication is broad within an organization. Personal motivation becomes part of the "formula" in organizational communica- tion, especially when the communication may be informal. Moreover, effective communication is affected by the degree to which it is re- ceived, or willing to be received.

The role of the receiver in organizational communication is a key. Messages are not *communicated* unless there is understanding of what those who send messages intend. This adds a dimension that some writ- ers and practitioners of management and administration ignore—the *ef- fective* individual relies on the degree of understanding and does not presume that the position of authority is enough to cause communica- tion to occur. That is, one does not infer that titular authority is suffi- cient for communication; the willingness of subordinates and colleagues to receive (and understand) messages is crucial.

People come into organizations as *independent* (freestanding and au- tonomous). As they become acculturated to and active within organiza- tions, they become *interdependent* (linked with, and possibly reliant upon, others). The effective person should "seek first to understand, then be understood" (Covey 1989). This wise advice leads to a discus- sion of empathic communication—understanding where others are as a key to connecting with them. "Few people have had any training in lis- tening" (238).

> Seeking to empathize first is converse to what individuals do typically. We . . . seek first to be understood. Most people do not listen with the intent to understand; they listen with the intent to reply. They're either speaking or preparing to speak. They're filtering everything through their own par- adigms, reading their autobiography into other people's lives. (Covey 1989, 239)

As we focus on our own filters and *needs* (see chapter 2), we process information through one of four levels, different from empathy: *ignor- ing* (not really listening), *pretending* (giving the appearance of listen- ing), *selective listening* (focusing only on parts of the conversation), or *attentive listening* (paying attention to the words that are being spoken and the nuances that accompany them). The highest form of listening is *empathic,* getting inside another person's frame of reference to understand that person's perspective (Covey 1989, 240).

Once you have understood another person, then you can move into your own frame and "seek to be understood." The power of empathy provides an entree and invitation for others to connect with you. (More will be said about this when we look at techniques of understanding, including reflection.)

Moving into the more specific context of education: "Effective leaders employ several principles of effective communication. One of the most important is the awareness that different individuals respond to different communication styles" (Morford and Willing 1993, 9). The negative outcome of failing to acknowledge and practice this precept is that "perceived lack of interpersonal sensitivity is a major factor in derailing leaders' careers" (9). Two other key principles are emphasized—the important link between trust and communication, leading to consistency, and understanding what the other person is really saying (supported by Covey's position).

Administrators confront crises (which are, perhaps, one step up from conflicts). These crises may be *personal* or related to *other individuals, groups, communications, finances,* or *major disasters.* Whether one confronts crises or conflicts, effectiveness is measured by the degree to which all parties are satisfied with the eventual decisions and outcomes—win/win, or I'm OK/You're OK.

Paul Salmon, former executive director of the American Association of School Administrators, provided commonsense guidelines for success in practical school administration: (1) ownership of the problem to be addressed (see "Whose monkey is it?" in the preface to this book); (2) the value of selective neglect; the importance of empowerment, enthusiasm, and effective communication; and (3) the need for positive reinforcement, cultivation of support, and good relations with primary and secondary stakeholders (Shannon 1994).

Education is organic, dynamic, and subject to the pressures and requirements of a changing society. One of the evolutionary aspects of education is a movement away from "parental" oversight (in many traditional organizations) to shared leadership and participatory decision making. (In some cases, this evolution is glacial, slow moving; in others, it is facilitated because of enthusiasm.) To empower and encourage this change, effective administrators are visible, communicate honestly, accept others, are open and genuine, face problems confidently, and seek appropriate solutions (Kerry and Murdoch 1993).

Conversely, "defective" schools are described, in part, by perquisites for the very few, faulty communication, adult-centered problems, interest-group indulgence, poor professional relationships, literal interpretation of technicalities, imperial leadership, incoherent evaluation procedures, loss of control, and low parental involvement (Gilman 1992). Failure to acknowledge the need for change and perseverance to hold too strongly to tradition, however outmoded, can doom schools and their administrators.

Field-based research has demonstrated an increasing awareness of necessary skills for new administrators. Conceptual self-awareness and people skills are viewed as eminently more important than technical skills (McGrevin and Schmieder 1993).

Communication, especially listening, is critical among the skills required for school administrators. Communication styles are one of the major areas of concern in administrator preparation (Pitner 1989). Administrator preparation programs should include opportunities for individuals to develop skills to communicate accurately and effectively by utilizing appropriate listening (Pohland, Milstein, Schilling, and Tonigan 1988, 58). "Careful analytical listening" (Peper 1989, 363) is the *first minimum skill* for the clinical education of school superintendents and principals. Skill in communication is the *most important competency* in terms of certification and employment of school administrators (Gousha and Mannan 1991).

The relationship between effective listening and satisfaction with supervision has been demonstrated. If staff perceive their principals to listen effectively, it predicts the degree to which they are satisfied with job supervision (Tackett 2000). Again, perception is the key. A positive perspective of one aspect generates a positive view of another. As conflict may be the *perception* of incompatible goals, so, too, is perception a strong factor in determining job satisfaction. (The preference for interacting with those who are similar is confirmed in other research [Knaupp n.d.].)

## Standards

A more recent emphasis for effective communication is found in the new standards for educational administration adopted by the Interstate School Leaders Licensing Consortium (ISLLC) and offered by the Educational Leadership Constituent Council (ELCC), which advises the National Council for the Accreditation of Teacher Education (NCATE), the recognized national accrediting body for educator preparation programs. Currently, thirty states and numerous other governmental entities are ISLLC members. The standards were adopted in 1996 with support from the Pew Educational Trust and the Danforth Foundation (CCSSO 2002). They were designed to guide preparation programs by specifying the knowledge, dispositions, and performance indicators for educational leaders.

Although these standards do not focus singly on communication, the outcomes of effective communication are embedded within the standards and their indicators. Examples of these emphases (in italics) are listed below (National Policy Board 2001):

Standard 1: Educational leaders . . . promote the success of all students by facilitating the development, *articulation*, implementation, and stewardship of a school or district vision of learning that is *shared* and supported by the school community.

Standard 2: Educational leaders . . . promote the success of all students by *advocating*, *nurturing*, and *sustaining* a school culture and instructional program conducive to student learning and staff professional growth.

Standard 4: Educational leaders . . . promote the success of all students by *collaborating* with family and community members, *responding* to diverse community interests and needs, and *mobilizing* community resources.

Standard 5: Educational leaders . . . promote the success of all students by *acting with integrity, fairness*, and *in an ethical manner*.

Standard 6: Educational leaders . . . have the knowledge and skills to promote the success of all students by *understanding, responding to*, and *influencing* the larger political, social, economic, legal, and cultural context.

Most specifically to the context of this book are the ISLLC *perform-ance indicators* relating to communication:

Standard 3: The administrator facilitates processes and engages in activities ensuring that . . .
- effective conflict resolution skills are used
- effective group-process and consensus-building skills are used
- effective communication skills are used

Standard 6: The administrator facilitates process and engages in activities
ensuring that . . .
- communication occurs among the school community concerning
trends, issues, and potential changes in the environment in which the
school operates. (CCSSO 2002)

The emphasis appears obvious: It is crucial that educational leaders
understand the messages that the various stakeholders in the educational enterprise want these leaders to understand and in the way they
want the messages understood. As a result, both preservice and in-service professional development of educational leaders should include direct and integrated preparation in specific and applied communication
skills.

These standards are broad-based and related to educational leadership in general ways. Some prefer to look at administrative qualifications
as they compare to former, tradition-based gender roles, where men are
the hunter-gatherers and women are the childbearing nurturers.

### Gender Myths and Realities

Certain issues relate specifically to women in administration—
networks and relationships and patterns of communication (Restine
1993). The issue of gender is interesting because of traditional role
models and perceived patterns of behavior and interaction. It is easy—
maybe too easy—to presume that because women are traditionally *nurturers*, all women prefer or demonstrate nurturing behavior before all
others (Stewart et al. 1990; Tannen 1990). Hence, some may presume
that women tend to effect a facilitative administrative style. Also, a similar presumption may be asserted about men: because men have assumed most leadership roles traditionally, *all* men are born leaders and

capable of demonstrating leadership traits as a function of gender. Men may have been viewed traditionally as being administratively authoritative. (I offer that this perspective limits possibilities that may be available to effective leaders, regardless of their gender. These assertions may suggest patterns in need of further examination; see chapter 2.)

The reality is that preferred patterns of communicating relate more to who people are personally rather than their gender. Some women prefer the *report* orientation attributed to men; some men seek *rapport*, a trait often ascribed to women (Tannen 1990). The needs we have guide us more than the gender stereotypes we have seen. In fact, these stereotypes may mislead us if we use them in a way that denies what we need. Confusion can arise: "Men don't cry" or "Nice girls don't do *that*."

### A Vision for the Future

Some of the impetus attached to the changing role of school administrators comes from initiatives in educational reform—school restructuring, role conflict, and changes in communication. When implemented, reforms suggest that administrators will facilitate increasingly shared governance, participant empowerment, and school-based decision making (Richardson et al. 1991). To be effective, these restructured functions have communication at their core.

While much of the reform efforts have focused on restructuring the participation of middle-level administrators—school-site managers and their colleagues—new or retooled patterns have been suggested for those at the top as well. Open communication is reported to be the key to success (Chance et al. 1991).

Educators are predominantly three (out of six possibilities; see chapter 3) types of people: those who are compassionate and want to help others; those who think the key to learning is the developing of clear thought patterns and logic; and those who believe that teaching the truth, important concepts, and values is the way to an educated populace. With regard to administrators, different resources are used to achieve desired goals through interaction according to their beliefs and values (the third type of educator mentioned above). Those who have ascended the administrative ladder held clear values, preferred influence to power, and utilized effective interpersonal and communication skills (Hall 1994). Wise administrators establish and maintain good communication with their staff, leading to trust and more effective administration (Lewis 1994).

Effective educational leaders focus on transactional communication, different sources of influence, and respect for the individual, all of which underpin a "blueprint" of the effort needed from each group of stakeholders in the educational venture (Schmuck and Schmuck 1992). When carrying this to the highest level of school governance—the policy making and planning that occurs between the school board and the administration—effective communication is the key to that relationship (American Association of School Administrators 1994). When this is translated into team building, employees are enabled to communicate in a way that facilitates effective team functioning (Southard 1993).

The implications are clear—effective communication is a requisite, if not the most important, skill area for effective educational leadership. The skills involved in effective communication should be part of the preservice preparation and part of the continuing professional development of school administrators. What is missing is a clear direction for this preparation. The next chapters will discuss specifics of effective communication, explicate a model—Process Communication (Kahler 1995)—that will allow educational leaders to achieve the goal of successful communication, and examine possibilities for educational leaders to refine their communication skills. Each of us is different and prefers different ways of experiencing the world—that is, to be effective, different builders use different tools.

## POINTS TO PONDER

- Communication is a requisite skill for effective educational leaders.
- More can be gained by *leading* than *bossing*.
- Traditional gender roles need to be reexamined.
- Communication occurs when understanding is present.

## REFERENCES

American Association of School Administrators. 1994. *Roles and relationships: School boards and superintendents.* Rev. ed. Arlington, Va.: American Association of School Administrators. ERIC, ED 371465.

Bargar, R. R., and R. L. Hoover. 1984. Psychological type and the matching of cognitive styles. *Theory into Practice* 23 (winter): 56–63.

Barker, J. L. 1999. *Leadershift: Five lessons for leaders in the twenty-first century.* St. Paul, Minn.: Star Thrower Productions. Video.

Barnard, C. I. 1938. *The functions of the executive.* Cambridge, Mass.: Harvard University Press.

Berne, E. 1964. *Games people play: The psychology of human relationships.* New York: Grove Press.

Bondesio, M. J. 1992. Conflict management at school: An unavoidable task. Paper presented at the regional conference of the Commonwealth Council for Educational Administration, August, Hong Kong. ERIC, ED 355655.

Chance, E. W., et al. 1991. Long-term rural superintendents: Characteristics and attributes. Paper presented at the annual convention of the National Rural Education Association, October, Jackson, Miss. ERIC, ED 339572.

Council of Chief State School Officers (CCSSO). 2002. *Interstate school leaders licensure consortium* at www.ccsso.org/isllc.html

Covey, S. R. 1989. *The seven habits of highly effective people: Powerful lessons in personal change.* New York: Simon and Schuster.

Ernst, F. 1973. Psychological rackets in the OK corral. *Transactional Analysis Journal* 3 (2): 19–23.

Gilbert, M. B. 1996. The process communication model: Understanding ourselves and others. *NASSP Bulletin* 80 (578): 75–80.

———. 1999. Why educators have problems with some students: Understanding frames of preference. *Journal of Educational Administration* 37: 243–55. ERIC, EJ 592943.

———. 2000. An analysis of factors related to school-district size in Arkansas. *Research in the Schools* 7 (2): 31–37.

Gilman, D. A. 1992. This issue: Correlates of a defective school. *Contemporary Education* 63 (2): 89–90. ERIC, EJ 447974.

Glasser, W. 1990. *The quality school: Managing students without coercion.* New York: Harper and Row.

Gousha, R. P., and G. Mannan. 1991. Analysis of selected competencies: Components, acquisition and measurement perceptions of three groups of stakeholders in education. Paper presented at the annual meeting of the National Council of Professors of Educational Administration, August, Fargo, N.D. ERIC, ED 336850.

Hall, V. 1994. Making a difference: Women headteachers' contribution to schools as learning institutions. Paper presented at the annual meeting of the British Educational Management and Administration Society, Manchester, England. ERIC, ED 376579.

Harris, A. B., and Harris, T. A. 1985. *Staying OK*. New York: Harper and Row.

Harris, T. A. 1969. *I'm OK—You're OK: A practical guide to transactional analysis*. New York: Harper and Row.

Hersey, P., K. Blanchard, and D. E. Johnson. 1996. *Management of organizational behavior: Utilizing human resources*. 7th ed. Englewood Cliffs, N.J.: Prentice-Hall.

Kagan, D. M., and D. J. Grandgenett. 1987. Personality and interaction analysis. *Research in Education* 12 (37): 13–24.

Kahler, T. 1995. *The process teaching seminars*. Little Rock, Ark.: Kahler Communications.

Kerry, T., and A. Murdoch. 1993. Education managers as leaders: Some thoughts on the context of the changing nature of schools. *School Organisation* 13: 221–30. ERIC, EJ 472566.

Knaupp, J. n.d. Preservice teachers' ranking of personality characteristics preferred by primary students, middle school students, parents and administrators. Unpublished paper, Arizona State University.

Lewis, P. M. 1994. Communication techniques: Building better relationships with academic personnel. *Business Officer* (February): 38–40. ERIC, EJ 477919.

McGregor, D. 1960. *The human side of enterprise*. New York: McGraw-Hill.

McGrevin, C. E., and J. H. Schmieder. 1993. Keys to success: Critical skills for the novice principal. Paper presented at the annual meeting of the American Educational Research Association, April, Atlanta, Ga. ERIC, ED 361852.

Morford, J. A., and D. Willing. 1993. Communication: Key to effective administration. *Adult Learning* (March/April): 9–10.

National Policy Board for Educational Administration. 2001. *New NCATE standards for educational administration* at www.npbea.org/NCATE_materials.html

Peper, J. B. 1989. Clinical education for school superintendents and principals: The missing link. In *Leaders for America's schools: The reports and papers of the national commission on excellence in educational administration*, edited by D. E. Griffiths, R. T. Stout, and P. B. Forsyth, 360–66. Berkeley, Calif.: McCutchan.

Pitner, N. J. 1989. School administrator preparation: The state of the art. In *Leaders for America's schools: The reports and papers of the national commission on excellence in educational administration*, edited by D. E. Griffiths, R. T. Stout, and P. B. Forsyth, 367–402. Berkeley, Calif.: McCutchan.

Pohland, P., M. Milstein, N. Schilling, and J. S. Tonigan. 1988. Emergent issues in the curriculum of educational administration. In *New directions for ad-*

*ministrator preparation*, edited by F. C. Wendel and M. T. Bryant, 37–61. Tempe, Ariz.: University Council for Educational Administration.

Restine, L. N. 1993. *Women in administration: Facilitators for change*. Newbury Park, Calif.: Corwin Press. ERIC, ED 358565.

Richardson, M. D., et al. 1991. The changing role of the school principal: A research synthesis. Paper presented at the annual meeting of the Mid-South Educational Research Association, November, Louisville, Ky. ERIC, ED 345320.

Schmuck, R. A., and P. A. Schmuck. 1992. *Small districts, big problems: Making school everybody's house*. Newbury Park, Calif.: Corwin Press. ERIC, ED 370747.

Shannon, T. A. 1994. Salmon's laws. *Executive Educator* (April): 52–54. ERIC, EJ 481340.

Simon, H. A. 1957. *Administrative behavior: A study of decision-making processes in administrative organization*. 2nd ed. New York: The Free Press.

Southard, S. 1993. Total quality management (Team building and cross training): From business to academe and back again to business. Paper presented at the annual meeting of the Conference on College Composition and Communication, March/April, San Diego, Calif. ERIC, ED 359567.

Stewart, L. P., A. D. Stewart, S. A. Friedley, and P. J. Cooper. 1990. *Communication between the sexes: Sex differences and sex-role stereotypes*. Scottsdale, Ariz.: Gorsuch Scarisbrick.

Tackett, J. D. 2000. Self-reported teacher job satisfaction and perceptions of administrative listening skills. Unpublished doctoral dissertation, University of Arkansas at Little Rock.

Tannen, D. 1990. *You just don't understand: Men and women in conversation*. New York: William Morrow.

# Two

## The Start of Communication

### LISTENING IN SCHOOL

The key to effective interaction is understanding what others want us to understand. As humans interacting with others, we communicate about 80 percent of each day. This means that most of our waking hours are spent writing, reading, speaking, or listening.

Pioneers in the field of listening—Paul Rankin (1928), Ralph Nichols and Leonard Stevens (1956), Lyman Steil (1984, 1991), and others— have said that listening is a skill taught inversely to its use. More specifically, the average person spends almost one half of each day in listening situations, while receiving little or no formal training in listening. Moreover, students are taught various components and nuances of writing all the way through formal schooling, yet this is a skill used only about 10 percent of the time.

So when do we learn how to listen? Many times the only listening training we receive is the check for attention: "Did you hear what I said?" Or the reminder that we are not listening: "I don't think you understand."

**Table 2.1    Listening Skills**

| Skill | Percentage Used | When Learned |
|---|:---:|:---:|
| Writing | 10 | Prekindergarten—Graduate |
| Reading | 15 | Prekindergarten—Grade 8 |
| Speaking | 30 | First six months of life |
| Listening | 45 | ? |

But what is listening? It "is the process of attending to, making meaning from and responding to spoken and/or nonverbal messages" (International Listening Association 1996).

Before we get into the more formal listening situations—such as in school or on the job—we may see ineffective listening by parents and other adults. When individuals encounter ineffective listening early in life and base their own listening on the patterns they experience, it is very difficult to change those patterns later.

In school, youngsters are captive and are expected to listen 65 to 90 percent of the time. Unless the school is exceptional and committed to listening education, much of the language arts instruction is focused on reading and writing. However, either the necessity for oral communication skills is ignored or there is a concerted effort to place the emphasis on reading and writing, skills used outside of school only 25 percent of the time. "Humans listen before they speak, speak before they read, and read before they write. Thus, failure to refine our listening skills impairs the entire process of human communication" (Wolff, Marsnik, Tacey, and Nichols 1983, 24).

Schools emphasize using reading and writing skills, but the prerequisite listening and speaking skills have not been taught as heavily, if at all. Learning styles may have been molded by this instructional emphasis. (The possible modes for learning are tactile/kinesthetic ["hands-on" learning by doing], visual, and auditory.) Because of the emphasis on reading and writing (and the bombardment of visual imagery in the world outside of school), most youngsters choose the visual mode (75 percent), much to the exclusion of the others (Gilbert 1984, 1988; see also Barbe and Swassing 1979). (It is important to acknowledge that reading skills allow people to learn independently.)

When confronted by the discrepancies between instructional time and use of language arts skills and asked why listening is not taught in the schools to any great extent, teachers responded similarly on three separate occasions (Steil 1984):

1. No one taught me how to teach listening (refer back to my first "Ah ha" in the preface).
2. There is not enough time in the school day.
3. There are not enough materials.

There is probably one additional consideration—no one taught teachers how to listen. Therefore, it would be somewhat unusual for teachers to be eager about teaching a skill, the components of which they might not know or with which they are uncomfortable.

The classroom teacher is the linchpin to formal listening instruction. Without a commitment to teaching listening as a skill, the teacher can impede learning in this critical communication skill. This does not negate the need for learning the other communication skills; it only suggests that there is a sharp imbalance between use and instruction.

However, the critical question is: What do we do about the workers of today who may suffer the outcomes of poor communication? Many people who lose their jobs do so because of the inability to communicate effectively. This does not only mean that the workers are to blame, only that the issue has dire need of being addressed.

### Some Problems in Teaching Listening

The atmosphere in which people learn to listen is important. When one attempts to teach good listening habits, it is necessary to structure an environment conducive to listening (Barker 1971):

1. Establish a comfortable, quiet, and relaxed atmosphere.
2. Make sure the audience knows (senses) the purpose for listening.
3. Prepare the listeners for what they are about to hear.
4. Break up long periods of listening with other activities.

Perhaps one of the most difficult things to accomplish in teaching listening is knowing whether the audience is indeed listening. However, whose responsibility is that? Consider that listening is the responsibility of the listener and the consequences of poor listening are the listener's.

It may not be appropriate for teachers to be passive in allowing students to be fully responsible for the outcomes of their listening. They should not presume that eye contact, "correct" posture, and stock responses to which divergent answers are not desired (e.g., "uh huh") are adequate indicators of effective listening. Students should be prompted to listen well. One incentive is a spotlight—an area in the classroom or an actual spotlight. When the teacher stands in the "spotlight," the students understand that an important message is forthcoming and will be delivered only once. The incentive is that if the student does not attend to the message, something important will be lost (Lundsteen 1979). For older students, the notion of "This will be on the test" usually gets their attention.

Some measures of listening are *summarizing, drawing inferences, recalling facts accurately,* and *recalling facts in sequence* (Barker 1971). Teachers may not wish to take the time to check for these measures; indeed, the typical classroom with thirty pupils is a near-impossible place in which to receive continual information about pupil progress in listening.

The point here is that listening is undertaught, and the consequences of poor listening are compounded within one's life. The effective educational leader should be sure that appropriate emphasis is given to listening instruction and reinforcement for careful listening throughout the organization.

### How Well Do Educators Listen?

Educators seem to listen better when compared to most other people. In one study, more than 300 educators from all levels exceeded the national mean in listening effectiveness by more than 15 percent (Gilbert 1997). These educators were least proficient in *following directions and instructions* and most proficient in *evaluating emotional responses in messages*. There were no distinctions in gender, whether they were in a school or college, what their position was, or if they worked in a public or independent organization; they listened with equal effectiveness. (Appendix B recounts a discussion of the statistical results of the study.)

Listening better than others is an interesting observation regarding educators. The need to listen effectively is critical to one's success—as a student, as a teacher, as an administrator, as a person. Although the results of the study seem to indicate that one group of educators outstripped the national norms in all but one category, it is noted that most people without an awareness of their listening effectiveness or the attendant skills could benefit greatly from listening training (compare tables 2.2 and 2.3 in this chapter).

### Is There a Future for Listening in School?

The concerns voiced by the teachers in the surveys done by Steil (1984)—(1) No one taught me how to teach listening; (2) There is not enough time in the school day; and (3) There are not enough materials—may not be as prevalent today. There are more opportunities for teachers to learn how to listen and how to teach listening, and there are many more materials. From many of the educational reform reports, there may be an impetus for listening to be added as an integral part of the curriculum. However, that impetus must come from within school districts as well; they might develop an organizational philosophy that includes listening as part of language arts reform (Gilbert 1984). Further, school administrators, at both the site and central office, must be supportive and encouraging. Moreover, they must lead their staffs into more effective listening behaviors, if they expect them to encourage better listening emphasis in their students.

To infuse listening training as part of any school curriculum, there must be a dedication and commitment of those who make and implement decisions to that training for any plan to succeed. Part of this commitment would be an in-service training program for current staff members, together with preservice training and orientation for new staff members.

To carry this idea further: schools and colleges of education might consider reorienting the language arts methods courses to focus more heavily on listening pedagogy as part of preservice professional education programs. If the newly trained professionals have learned how to teach listening as part of their teaching preparation programs, then they might be instrumental in affecting languages arts emphases in the districts in which they work.

To start on a small and independent scale, educators might make a commitment to change their own listening habits (and encourage others to follow their lead). Some suggestions for improvement are as follows (Lyle 1984):

1. Realize that listening takes real effort: Be prepared to expend time and energy.
2. Look at the person who is speaking to you: Do not fake attention or seem uninterested.

3. Turn off feelings as much as possible and listen with an open mind: Receive information as fresh; suppress your bias.
4. Do not jump to conclusions; hear the person out: Do not interrupt.
5. Separate fact from inference.
6. Listen between the lines to hear what is not being said: Are you getting all the information?
7. Learn to read nonverbal communication: What are the person's posture and movements telling you?
8. Pay attention to the feedback you provide: Have you confirmed, corrected, or clarified your understanding of the message?

There are few who would question the importance of effective communication. The key to change in current practice in many places is for those in positions of decision making to recognize the need and to address that need. The information presented here may raise the questions to be answered and may provide the basis for change for those who wish to do so. These ideas also underpin how we can become effective educational leaders.

## LISTENING TO COMMUNICATE

Communicating is conveying a message that is understood by others in the way you intend. Messages pass through various screens as they are received. These screens may muddle messages and their understanding. Prior experiences, feelings, beliefs, physical state, and conflicting agenda all may serve to lead one in a direction different from what the sender intends. Figure 2.1 shows the communication process (adapted from Steil [1984]).

To check for understanding, the message is looped from sender to receiver and back again. Additionally, one has a better chance of communicating if the time, place, and context are appropriate. If it is the wrong time or place or situation, the process may be confounded. Trying to tell something to a colleague during an important meeting when she has just come from the doctor's office with heavy news is not likely to be successful, even though the message may be simple.

## COMMUNICATION PROCESS

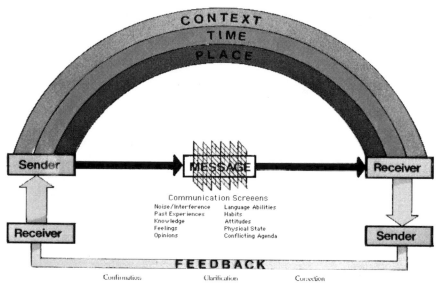

**Figure 2.1   Communication Rainbow**

*The Key*

The most critical communication skill, listening, is the one that is taught the least. In fact, most people receive little or no formal training in the techniques of listening.

Adults are asked to listen about one half of the time (Rankin 1928), yet the average listener can recall only 50 percent of a message immediately after it has been delivered. This rate drops to 25 percent in a very short period. Therefore, the average person may be *75 percent ineffective* as a listener (Steil, Barker, and Watson 1983). If asked, most people would support the idea of listening as an important, if not critical, skill, but becoming a proficient listener may be something for *others* to do, much like observing the speed limits on the highways.

Many hold some misconceptions about listening.

1. Listening is a matter of intelligence.
2. Good hearing and good listening are closely associated.
3. Listening is an automatic reflex.

4. Daily practice eliminates the need for training in listening.
5. Learning to read will automatically improve listening.
6. Learning to read is more important than learning to listen.
7. The speaker is totally responsible for success in oral communication.
8. Listening is essentially passive.
9. Listening means agreement.
10. The consequences of careless listening are minimal. (Wolff, Marsnik, Tacey, and Nichols 1983)

What is actual is what occurs when "not" is added to each of the above statements. Because many do not understand fully what listening is and what listening is not, bad habits continue.

People who receive listening training perform at significantly higher levels than those who do not. The implications for education are clear—*those who listen better, do better.*

### How Administrators Listen

Principals believe they are moderately good listeners. They see themselves as attentive and understanding but note they may be distracted when their interest wanes, may presume to understand without checking back, or may allow feelings about a speaker to interfere. Related research using school principals as sample administrators is arrayed in this chapter; table 2.2 shows general perceptions (Gilbert 1984). Principals saw themselves proficient in understanding messages, being able to stay focused, and being able to sort through details for the overall message. Conversely, they indicated they had problems with attending when their interest waned, when they were distracted by the delivery or appearance of the speaker, and that they tended to try to understand a message (too?) quickly.

To reiterate: Communication occurs when the listener understands a message in the same way the speaker intended that it be understood. Failure to employ feedback—to confirm, clarify, or correct a message—can lead to misunderstanding.

Barriers to listening effectiveness—*being distracted, not being ready to listen, anticipation, interrupting, planning for a response,* and *think-*

**Table 2.2   Principals' Listening Behaviors Perceptions**

Most Proficient

1. I **rarely** don't understand, so I quit listening.
2. It is **rarely** hard for me to keep up with a message because I can't figure out what might come next and I lose interest.
3. I **rarely** get so concerned with details that I have difficulty separating the key ideas from those that are only supporting.
4. I **rarely** find myself distracted easily, so I miss part of the message and cannot figure out what is going on.

Least Proficient

1. I **sometimes** don't pay attention when I'm not interested in the subject.
2. My response to an oral message is **frequently** based on my initial understanding of that message.
3. I **sometimes** judge speakers mainly on delivery style and appearance.

Note: With respect to item 2 under "Least Proficient," responses based on initial understanding might be faulty if one does not check for accuracy.

*ing of other things*—can get in the way of interacting successfully. Most principals perceived their own listening behaviors to be effective; however, their staffs noted differences in how the principals perceive themselves and how they see their principals (Gilbert 1989). There is consensus on two areas of proficiency and deficiency. Table 2.3 shows the agreement (Gilbert 1989).

Staff indicated that their principals understood what they had to say and could stay focused. However, they also perceived that their principals might be distracted by preparing their own responses, especially if they were in disagreement with staff, and might not probe deeply enough for full understanding of the staff member's message.

**Table 2.3   Staff Perceptions of Principals' Listening**

Most Proficient

1. Principals **rarely** don't understand and quit listening.
2. Principals **rarely** find it hard to keep up with a message because they can't figure out what might come next and lose interest.

Least Proficient

1. Principals **sometimes** get wrapped up in their own argument and planning for a response.
2. Principals' responses are **sometimes** based on initial understanding.

Staff members may assess their supervisor's overall performance as a supervisor in looking at the listening behaviors—that is, there may be a performance "halo." If the overall performance is perceived as being good, any subset of that performance, such as listening, is seen in the same light. Also, staff might agree that their supervisors listen well if they grant requests—"If you give me what I want, then I know you have listened carefully. Conversely, if you do not give me what I ask for, then you obviously do not understand my request." Of course, understanding and compliance are not always closely linked.

> I remember an interaction I had with one of my daughters. She had asked me for something; I denied her request. She asked again—still no positive response from me. She then pouted, "You just don't understand!"
>
> Of course, this was a challenge to someone who had done substantial work with communication. I responded by clarifying my understanding of what she wanted.
>
> "Is that right?" I asked.
>
> "Yes," she said, surprised.
>
> "Then it's not that I don't understand. It's just that I am not giving you what you want."
>
> She turned and huffed away.

The point here is that *understanding* does not mean agreement, and lack of agreement may be construed as poor listening or ineffective communicating.

Another interesting offshoot is that principals who were currently unmarried (either divorced or widowed) were perceived to listen less well than those who were married or who had never married (Gilbert 1989). One speculation might be that the trauma of the principal's former marital situation caused principals to listen less well (and possibly to be less effective in other interpersonal behaviors). The obverse is also possible—that ineffective communication and other interpersonal behaviors caused the dissolution of the marriage (as might be suggested by marriage counselors). A cautious interpretation is: principals who listen more effectively are either married or never have been married.

Another focus might be principals' listening considering the job satisfaction of teachers. Teachers' perceptions of administrative listening are a predictor of teachers' self-reported job satisfaction with supervision (Tackett 2000).

How principals listen can have a notable impact on their staffs. That is, principals who are perceived to listen well relate more positively to their staffs.

### How to Listen Better

Although the need to be an effective listener may be apparent to principals and others in the school organization and in the community at large, what might be done to improve? Since listening is a skill, one might consider these steps for improving skills:

- Understand the *need* for the skill.
- *Learn* the component steps.
- *Practice* the steps.
- Receive *feedback* on how well the skill is being performed.
- *Incorporate* the skill and its components into your repertoire.

Repeated research has looked at the need for developing listening skills. Educational leaders are but one group who might benefit from improving their listening. To put the meat on the bones of this learning skeleton, here are some keys to effective listening:

1. Find areas of interest: Look for benefits and opportunities; ask "What's in this for me?"
2. Judge content, not delivery: Overlook delivery errors and concentrate on the main message.
3. Hold your fire: Withhold judgment until the message is complete.
4. Listen for ideas: Focus on central themes.
5. Be flexible: Take appropriate notes, adapting to the speaker's style. (Of course, one should get into the habit of taking notes and not rely on memory. One's memory may not be as reliable as one desires.)
6. Work at listening: Exhibit active body readiness—eye contact,

supportive facial expressions, and so forth. Ask clarifying questions and respond appropriately.

7. Resist distractions: Fight or avoid distractions; tolerate bad habits
   in others; know how to concentrate (and recognize when concen-
   tration is waning or absent).
8. Exercise your mind: Search for challenging material.
9. Keep your mind open: Know your emotional triggers and be prepared to combat their control over you.
10. Capitalize on the fact that *thought* is faster than *speech*: Chal-
    lenge (mentally), anticipate, summarize, and reflect on what has
    been said; weigh the evidence; listen between the lines. (Nichols
    and Stevens 1956; Steil, Barker, and Watson 1983)

### Leading to More Effective Listening

With the hue and cry for excellence in the schools, principals and district administrators might want to address a persistent and vaguely recognized problem—students may not know how to listen because they
have not been taught how. They have not been taught how because
their teachers have not been taught how to teach listening and may not
be good listeners themselves. The emphasis in teacher preparation programs and in language arts curricula has been on written communication (writing and reading) to the exclusion of oral communication (listening and speaking), yet oral communication is needed and used about
75 percent of the time in the world outside the school. The leadership
for a change in emphasis can come from the principal and can be transmitted throughout the school organization.

If the school-site or central-office administrator is (or becomes) a proficient and effective listener, then a model is established for other staff
members to do the same. If the staff recognizes the value of listening
well and can exhibit the skill, a major hurdle in the barrier to getting
others to attend *mentally* will be overcome.

For example, students are placed in listening situations for 65 to 90
percent of the instructional day. If they do not know how to listen and
are not taught how to listen, then much of what goes on in the classroom
may be *lost* or *need to be repeated*.

Do principals listen well? They think that they do . . . but there are areas for improvement, especially in *barriers to effective listening*. The keys to effective listening provide means for improving listening behaviors. The roadblock in incorporating these suggestions is in understanding that a problem exists. The emphasis on listening as a crucial skill is not widespread; moreover, a potential problem might be masked by other interpersonal or organizational behavior deficiencies. Educators who model and transmit good listening behaviors can go a long way to improving relationships and to becoming more effective leaders.

### Reflective Listening

People want to talk more than they listen. In conversations, many think that controlling the interchange is the way to get one's point across and direct or persuade others. Establishing rapport that leads to understanding may be a more productive way to proceed. (I contend that this rapport is genderless, contrary to the assertion that rapport is a female goal [Tannen 1990]. While feeling-oriented people are decidedly female, they are not exclusively so. See the description of Feelers in chapter 3.)

The feedback loop depicted in the Communication Rainbow (figure 2.1) is a way to ensure that understanding has happened. Confirming, correcting, or clarifying a message are ways to verify the understanding. Another way to describe this aspect of communication is through *reflection*.

In reflective listening, we try to convey to the sender that we have understood—that she or he has communicated. We are looking for agreement of interpretation, not necessarily agreement of content. What we, as listeners, want is the sender to get to "Yes! That's it! You got it!" We paraphrase what we have heard in thought (and possibly feeling) until we get to "Yes!" (Bolton 1979).

Part of the problem in turning ourselves outward to another perspective is that we have to *want* to understand and to *put aside* our own needs to accomplish that understanding. Some may think that "Yes!" means agreement. If we have a different point of view or position, we may want to push our views or be unwilling to accept (not agree with) another idea or belief. To understand another means that we have to "listen" to the message from someone else's perspective. To do this implies we have common "screens" (ways of filtering the message) and are willing to be empathic, or at least *shift*. (This notion of shifting will be expanded later.)

While *empathy* usually speaks to understanding how another feels, it may also describe looking at issues through another's eyes (screens), or walking the same path. The emphasis is staying receptive in order to understand. "Communication between persons . . . (is) a mysterious business that . . . is almost never achieved except in part" (Rogers 1970, 11).

Understanding another is empowering for both you and the other person. You have opened yourself to "hear" truly and build a relationship. The other person has connected when he or she has been understood. There is a sense of satisfaction when communication occurs; however, we are not always successful.

### Are You Listening to Me?

While we know there are measures to check if another *has listened*, we do not know at any moment if someone else *is listening*. We cannot get into someone's head to *see* if indeed they are attending to what we are saying . . . or to something else.

Of course, we can observe attentive body language—eye contact, alert posture, and so on—to determine if our communication partner is prepared to listen, but we do not know if they *are* listening. We can ask questions to check for understanding. We can determine if their responses are contextually accurate, but we do not *know* that listening is occurring. We can only determine if accurate listening has happened *after the fact*—when they have done what we have asked or directed, or if their responses reflect what we have wanted them to understand.

When the messages are not spoken or delivered at different times, our listening checks may be confounded. Newer technology has added greater opportunities for communicating and potential for greater "garbling."

### Dealing with "Cyberspeak"

Listening is accomplished best when we are face-to-face, either with one person or a group of people. In this age of burgeoning technology, we can also hear and listen to others via telephone conversations and voice mail/messaging. What we give up on the phone is the "body language" or nonverbal cues that are most helpful when we look at someone. In person, we might see their joy, instead of just listening to their excitement. We might note the tapping of a foot or pencil to indicate impatience, frustration, or nervousness. Clear electronic transmission does not mean effective communication—that is, determining the receiver understood what was intended. (It will be interesting to see how a possible proliferation of videophones may add the nonverbal aspects to telephonic communication.)

We further confound communication by making use of what might be called "cyberspeak"—electronic mail (e-mail), chat rooms, and instant messaging. We can talk to and with others synchronously (in a time-specific way, as in face-to-face conversation) or asynchronously (at different times, much in the way we respond to posted mail). The problem with asynchronous messaging is that we lose any vocal qualities, in addition to the loss of visual cues. These losses increase the possibility of misunderstanding—hence, lack of communication, or the increased potential of miscommunication.

Sometimes, our correspondents try to help using "cybercode." When someone wants to indicate smiling or being humorous, he may use "lol" (for "laughing out loud") or visual (punctuation) code—emoticons—[:)], which looks like a smiling face when rotated clockwise. These and many other codes are used to offset the visual and other nonverbal cues we use to understand each other in face-to-face interaction.

Being able to "converse" with someone at different times is convenient. It means we do not have to set appointments for mutually available times to meet. We can take care of business in whatever sequence suits us.

Being able to communicate quickly, in different modes, and using convenient preferences allows us to be in touch with others how and when we want. The problem (but some might call it an advantage) with distant communication is that we can avoid confrontation, according to our needs and preferences. If we have to address conflict with another person, some might prefer to avoid doing it, or at least avoid doing it face-to-face. This may provide some protection for those in organizationally unequal positions or highly emotional circumstances.

So the effectiveness of communicating depends on accurate transmission of a message (with all of the possible glitches that can occur) and the willingness of a person to *listen*. The effective leader has learned how to communicate well. This ability to understand what others want us to understand affirms our leadership.

"If one knows how to listen, one can learn even from those who speak badly." (Plutarch)

## POINTS TO PONDER

- Listening is a much-used but undertaught communication skill.
- Listening can be improved with practicing effective techniques.
- Modeling effective listening by educational leaders is important to placing emphasis on listening within the organization.
- Reflection is a key to ensuring that messages are understood—that is, communication has occurred.
- Electronic technology provides new challenges for communicating effectively.

## REFERENCES

Barbe, W. B., and R. H. Swassing. 1979. *Teaching through modality strengths.* Columbus, Ohio: Zaner-Bloser.

Barker, L. L. 1971. *Listening behavior.* Englewood Cliffs, N.J.: Prentice-Hall.

Bolton, R. 1979. *People skills: How to assert yourself, listen to others, and resolve conflicts.* Englewood Cliffs, N.J.: Prentice-Hall.

Gilbert, M. B. 1984. Listening in the schools. In *Directions in education: Perspectives for the twenty-first century,* edited by M. B. Gilbert, 57–69. Stockton, Calif.: University of the Pacific, Bureau of Educational Research and Field Services/Phi Delta Kappa, District II.

———. 1988. Listening in school: I know you can hear me—but are you listening? *Journal of the International Listening Association* 2: 121–32.

———. 1989. Perceptions of listening behaviors of school principals. *School Organisation* 9: 271–82.

———. 1997. An examination of the listening effectiveness of educators: Performance versus preference. Presentation at the annual convention of the International Listening Association, March, Mobile, Ala.

Lundsteen, S. W. 1979. *Listening: Its impact on reading and the other language arts*. Urbana, Ill.: National Council of Teachers of English.

Lyle, M. 1984. Teaching listening skills for parents. Presentation at the annual convention of the International Listening Association, March, Scottsdale, Ariz.

Nichols, R., and L. Stevens. 1956. *Are you listening?* New York: McGraw-Hill.

Rankin, P. 1928. The importance of listening ability. *English Journal* 17: 623–30.

Rogers, C. R. 1970. Being in relationship. *Voices* (fall): 11–19.

Steil, L. K. 1984. The ILA and the certification of teachers and trainers. Presentation at the annual convention of the International Listening Association, March, Scottsdale, Ariz.

———. 1991. Listening through our driving forces: A strategy for developing the complete listener. Presentation at the twelfth annual convention of the International Listening Association, March, Jacksonville, Fla.

Steil, L. K., L. L. Barker, and K. W. Watson. 1983. *Effective listening: Key to your success*. Reading, Mass.: Addison-Wesley.

Tackett, J. D. 2000. Self-reported teacher job satisfaction and perception of administrative listening skills. Unpublished doctoral dissertation, University of Arkansas at Little Rock.

Tannen, D. 1990. *You just don't understand: Men and women in conversation*. New York: William Morrow.

Wolff, F. I., N. Marsnik, W. Tacey, and R. Nichols. (1983). *Perceptive listening*. New York: Holt, Rinehart and Winston.

# THREE

## Communication Blueprints:
## Different Tools for Different Builders

People have differing communication styles and ways of processing information. Most models are based on aspects of one's preferences for taking in or giving out information, or both.

Preference for information input may be one of three modes—visual, kinesthetic (hands-on or tactile), or auditory. Personality or learning characteristics may be related to (1) communication styles and preferences, according to four scales: extraversion-introversion, sensing-intuition, thinking-feeling, and judging-perceiving (Myers and Briggs 1943, 1976, 1985), (2) colors, as descriptors of preferences (de Bono 1985; Keirsey and Bates 1984; Noland 1978), (3) degrees of specificity or structure (Gregorc 1982), or (4) environment or subject matter (Gardner 1983). In sum, we communicate depending on one or several aspects of personality and individual tendencies in life and in professional situations.

## PERSONALITY MODELS

The different models all seem to focus on the preferences people have for processing information and interacting with others. Almost all of the models describe the current state of people. That is, we see various characteristics that are determined by a person's responses to an instrument or by an observation of how things are *currently*.

The identifiers shown in table 3.1 demonstrate the comparisons between the models related to education. *Only* the Kahler (1982b) model (described in greater detail below), Process Communication, indicates the *current* state *and* if an individual has experienced a change in preferences. Process Communication also shows the potential a person has to interact easily and effectively with others who are different. This model provides a toolbox with a myriad of tools for different situations.

The Process Communication Model (PCM) (Kahler 1982b) describes six personality types, drawing on transactional analysis concepts (Berne 1964), with historical underpinnings from Karl Jung and Alfred Adler. No one personality type is better or worse, more or less OK, more or less intelligent. According to Kahler, one's personality structure resembles a six-story condominium, where the first floor represents the foundation—strongest personality type—and where each remaining floor represents the other personality types in order of the strength of each. This generated order of personality types is firmly established about age seven, and the ability to move to these different "floors" of our personality is measurable and predictable. One can access the different floors by going up or coming down in an "elevator."

Each personality type has a different set of needs, perceptions, and behaviors that influences how we interact with others and the world in which we live. This multidimensional approach is a major asset of the PCM. The *condominium* analogy is quite apt because it suggests we *own* our personality and, moreover, it is paid for—no mortgage or lien.

**Table 3.1  Comparative Personality Indicators**

| Kahler | Myers/ Briggs | Gregorc | De Bono | McCarthy | Keirsey/ Bates | Gardner |
|---|---|---|---|---|---|---|
| Reactor | E*FJ | CA | Red Hat | Style One | | Interpersonal |
| Workaholic | **TJ | CS | Black Hat | Style Two | Gold | Logical-Mathematical |
| Persister | **TJ | CS | Blue Hat | Style Two | Green | Spatial; Linguistic |
| Dreamer | I*TP | CR | White Hat | | Blue | Intrapersonal |
| Rebel | EN*P | AR | Green Hat | Style Four | Orange | Musical; Bodily-Kinesthetic |
| Promoter | *NT* | CR | Yellow Hat | Style Three | | Bodily-Kinesthetic |

Myers-Briggs Identifiers:
E = Extraverted; F = Feeling; I = Introverted; J = Judging; N = Intuitive; P = Perceptive; T = Thinking

Gregorc Delineators:
A = Abstract; C = Concrete; R = Random; S = Sequential

However, it does require some maintenance. One *example* of a personality condominium is found in figure 3.1.

The person represented by the condominium in figure 3.1 is said to be a *base* Thinker, with Thinker being the "ground floor." This is the strongest part of this individual's personality. You will note that with each successive floor the amount of "furnishings" (relative energy) is equal to or less than the floor beneath it. This "energy" depicts what the individual has at his or her disposal to be able to interact with others. For the person exemplified in figure 3.1, there is sufficient energy to interact with Thinkers and Feelers, with Believers not too far behind. Funsters, Doers, and Dreamers would present more of a challenge.

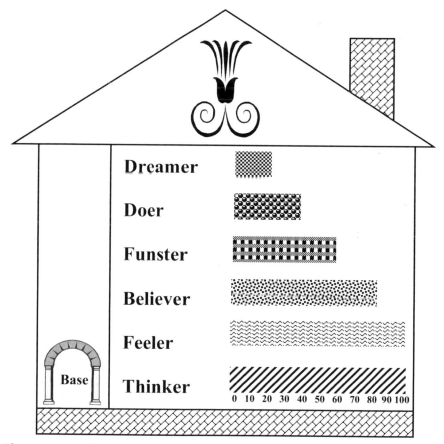

**Figure 3.1    Sample Base Personality Condominium**

Most people limit how they process reality by using only one or two of the six available floors of their personality structure. The PCM proposes that recognizing diverse personality types, needs (motivators), and negative behavior (distress) sequences is the key to effective communication and success.

The words, tones, postures, gestures, and facial expressions one uses indicate what one prefers. You will learn what these are as you examine the sample personalities in the following chapters. For example, Feelers would use a lot of feeling-laden terms: "I love your outfit." "I am so happy today." "How are you feeling?" Their tones would be warm and welcoming. Their gestures would be sensitive and inviting. Their posture would be open and nurturing. Their facial expressions would reflect their emotions.

Personalized profiles can be generated from a questionnaire validated for purposes of determining an individual's personality structure. These profiles include what one's motivators are, how one takes in and gives out information, and a reliable prediction of the negative behaviors a person will manifest when in distress. This aspect of predictable distress, also the need to measure compatibility, is why the PCM has been used by National Aeronautics and Space Administration (NASA) in the selection and training of astronauts (Kahler 1982a). These profile reports are valid for educators (Kahler 1996c), as well as for students, ages eleven to eighteen (Kahler 1996b).

## AN OVERVIEW OF PROCESS COMMUNICATION

The following describes each personality type (Kahler 1982b, 2000):

- Feelers are *warm, compassionate, and sensitive*; they like conversation and group-oriented activities. They show their emotions, like to please, and know they are appreciated. Feelings are their forte. (Thirty percent of the North American population has Feeler base personalities; mainly female—75 percent.)
- Thinkers are *responsible, logical, and organized*; they think before they feel and would rather be recognized than appreciated. (Twenty-five percent; mainly male—75 percent.)

- Believers are *observant, conscientious, and dedicated*; they prefer being alone or working one on one. They have strong beliefs about how a job should be done. (Ten percent; mainly male—75 percent.)
- Funsters are *spontaneous, creative, and playful*; they react with likes and dislikes and in distress do not answer questions directly. They need fun, attention, and active involvement. They prefer stimulating environments and like active people. (Twenty percent; mainly female—60 percent.)
- Doers are *resourceful, adaptable, and charming*; they adapt their behavior to the situation. They need immediate rewards and prefer exciting, stimulating activities. They learn by doing, not by feeling or thinking. (Five percent; mainly male—60 percent.)
- Dreamers are *imaginative, reflective, and calm*; they usually are passive and are absorbed with their thoughts. They seldom initiate conversations and start withdrawing when there is too much activity around them. (Ten percent; mainly female—60 percent.)

Note: The descriptors used here (with permission) are Kahler's terms in his Process Teaching Model, when identifying students (1996b), shown in the comparative indicators in table 3.1. Within the context of educational leadership and work with students, these terms seemed to fit more appropriately.

| | | |
|---|---|---|
| Feeler | — | Reactor |
| Thinker | = | Workaholic |
| Believer | = | Persister |
| Dreamer | = | Dreamer |
| Funster | = | Rebel |
| Doer | = | Promoter |

The intriguing/disturbing conclusion that can be drawn from an examination of personality types is that people, in education and elsewhere, whose needs are not met are going to have difficulties in learning and in meeting performance expectations. For example, a Funster student is very distractible and *needs* to have fun. If the learning activity is not "fun" (too repetitive or structured), the Funster may respond "I just don't get it" as a way of drawing the teacher into playing with him. (In PCM parlance, this is called a "try hard" *driver* [Kahler and Capers 1974], the first degree of predictable distress.) A teacher who is not predisposed to spend the extra energy required to meet a Funster's needs (or who may not have much Funster energy to draw upon) may suppose that the Funster is stupid, slow, or immature. This may mean that the Funster does not perform as expected and fails the activity, the unit, or the course.

Another example of a potential communication problem may be a Feeler teacher assigned to a Thinker principal. The Feeler needs sensory things (like pleasing colors, aromas, or family pictures) and must feel accepted as a person by others. The Thinker is predisposed to efficiency and may see sensory things as frivolous and unimportant. The Thinker is also task oriented and may not have (make) the time for the pleasantries and "stroking" needed by the Feeler. Should the Thinker consider praising someone, that praise is likely to be couched in terms of *his psychological need* of recognition of work (Kahler 1982a)—"Good job! You've increased test scores by 10 percent." Since Feelers need unconditional recognition as *people*, the teacher might say to herself, "Why does he just only see my work? I want to be liked and appreciated as a person. Colleagues and students aren't just coworkers and pupils to me; they're my extended family."

Not having received the unconditional acceptance needed, the Feeler may make mistakes (being *driven* by a "please you" state of mind—the first degree of distress). The Thinker concludes that praising does not work and begins to judge this person negatively.

## THE PCM IN ACTION

Communication occurs when the listener understands the speaker in the way the speaker wants to be understood. The other side, *miscommunication*, is that we do not communicate when the listener does not accept the offer or *channel* of communication (Kahler 1979).

Responding is the capstone (see epilogue) of most interactions—understanding the message and processing it to a response completes the communication event. In responding, the listener becomes the speaker and vice versa. Yet it is crucial that the response match the needs and perceptions of the individuals for communication to occur.

An example of processing the message and responding appropriately is found in the PCM through the components of perceptions and channels of communication.

### Perceptions

Each personality type has different perceptions to experience the environment and the world (Kahler 1982a).

Feelers—emotions
Thinkers—thoughts
Believers—opinions
Dreamers—inactions (reflections)
Funsters—reactions (likes and dislikes)
Doers—actions

These filters or screens provide the preferences for one's views and can be heard in the terms one uses.

Feelers will use emotional terms: "love," "sad," "happy," and so forth.
Thinkers will be logical: "ideas," "facts," "deadlines," and so on.
Believers will share opinions and beliefs: "important," "valuable," "committed," and similar terms.
Dreamers will be reflective: "It seems to me that . . ." "The ideas appear sound . . ." and similar phrases.
Funsters will react: "I like it!" "I hate this project!" and like responses.
Doers will focus on getting things done: "Bottom line," "Go for it!" and the like.

When we need or want to access different aspects of who we are because a person or situation invites us, we tap into that part of our personality that matches those perceptions.

| When I want to . . . | I access my |
|---|---|
| • be logical or structured | Thinker |
| • state my opinions or values | Believer |
| • feel or sense | Feeler |
| • reflect or imagine | Dreamer |
| • be creative or react | Funster |
| • act or be directive | Doer |

Most of us will prefer only one or two perceptions on a regular basis. These choices are based on the amount of continual access. That is, the more frequently we tap into a perception, the more familiar it becomes to us and the more adept we are in its use. Some people do not access some of the potential perceptions much or at all.

## Channels

Even if one does not know what people's personalities are, their responses will give meaningful clues into what their channels and perceptions are. Communication occurs between the different personality parts—*Protector, Sensor, Director, Computer, Comforter,* and *Emoter.* We communicate through five channels, identifiable by specific words, tones, gestures, and postures:

- *Channel One* (Interventive) offers directives, imperatives, or commands aimed at the senses (touch, smell, taste, hearing, or sight). The Interventive Channel is very useful when people are getting "out of control"; it helps them regain their composure and is useful in emergencies—"Stop! Take a breath!" It offers a message from one's Protector to be received by another's Sensor in an attempt to help the other person regain control.
- *Channel Two* (Directive) offers a command, imperative, or directive, and another person accepts this offer rationally or logically, responding crisply as a computer would in taking the command— "Make five copies of that memo and distribute it to the faculty." The offer comes from the Director part and is aimed at another's Computer (clear thinking part which focuses on a simple exchange of information).

- *Channel Three* (Requestive) involves the exchange of information, clearly and crisply—"Will you have your lesson-plan book available on your desk for the substitute teacher?" One's Computer request for information from another's Computer. The expectation is that the response will be simple and direct.
- *Channel Four* (Nurturative) offers from the warm, nurturing, caring, sensitive part, inviting someone else to feel cared for—"I appreciate your being part of our school family. It's nice to see you." The Comforter offers nurturance to be accepted by the other's Emoter.
- *Channel Five* (Emotive) involves an exchange from the reactive side of each person; it helps people stay receptive, creating a non-threatening and childlike atmosphere—"Wow! You really did a super job in knocking out that project." The offer and acceptance is between two Emoters, the responsive parts of people's personalities.

Each personality type has preferences for which channel will be most appropriate. Dreamers are directable, and Doers like action (the "bottom line"); they prefer the *directive* Channel Two. Thinkers and Believers are task oriented; they prefer the *requestive* Channel Three. Feelers want to *feel* first; they prefer the *nurturative* Channel Four. And Funsters are driven by likes and dislikes (reactions); they prefer to communicate first through the *emotive* Channel Five.

| *Channel* | *Personality* |
|---|---|
| 1. Interventive | All |
| 2. Directive | Dreamer, Doer |
| 3. Requestive | Believer |
| 4. Nurturative | Thinker, Feeler |
| 5. Emotive | Funster |

We tend to offer our own preferred personality channel predominantly (found in our personality base, or ground floor) and accompanying view of the world (perception) to others. For example, if I want to communicate and I am a Thinker, much of what I say will be couched in terms of ideas and thoughts. If I say, "Do you *think* that is a good *idea*?" then I have used a requestive channel and advertised my perceptual bias of the world—thoughts. If I am addressing a Feeler, I have missed that person's channel and perception. This will be heard in a response such as "I *feel* good about it." However, the Feeler can move to the Computer part of her personality to communicate with the Thinker, even if that is not her preference or strongest part—but she first must have gotten energized in her strongest parts in order to be able to move.

Responses from the other types might be:

"I *believe* it is a good idea," for Believers;
"I *like* it," for Funsters;
"*It's* okay," for Dreamers; and
"Okay! *Go for it!*" for Doers.

If leaders know the proper channels and perceptions for communicating with their staff, they can help with understanding the message and encouraging the desired behavior. For example, telling a Feeler that the proposed instructional unit is not appropriate for the school district at this time might begin with, "I am really glad that you are a member of our staff. I enjoy working with you." This allows the Feeler to receive the message in his or her strongest channel (nurturative) and perception (feelings/emotions) before, "I am sorry that we will not be able to approve your proposal now." A Thinker supervisor would, by nature, give only the rationale (logic), but the introductory statement of personal acceptance would reinforce the relationship with an acknowledged people person, who will hear the rest of the content through nurturing filters. Therefore, communication will occur—the receiver accepting the channel and understanding the message. Attempting to force individuals to accept a channel and bias, which are not theirs, will result in misunderstanding and miscommunication.

I remember a PCM workshop I was facilitating with a school staff. They had all completed the PCM inventory and received their individual profiles. The focus was the basic concepts of PCM.

As with many workshops, concepts are presented intensely. If the concepts are relatively new to the participants, there is a lot to absorb in a short period of time.

At one point in the second day, one Believer said she was a bit confused and asked me to "bring it down to my level." I was feeling a bit playful and knelt in front of her, asking "Is this better?" She literally *growled* at me.

Someone with a lot of Funster energy would have been energized with my playfulness, but this Believer was not amused. She had asked me a direct question (requestive channel), seeking specific information. She expected a direct answer. When she did not get it, she began to get into distress with her "You have to be perfect to be OK" driver.

It was an excellent example of miscommunication. I used it to demonstrate how I had failed to communicate—there was an offer of a message with no acceptance and in the wrong channel. (I wish I could say I had planned the interaction, but I had not.)

## MOTIVATION

### Needs

Each of us has needs. Abraham Maslow (1954) described them in categories from basic biological needs to higher-level psychological and social needs. Process Communication (Kahler 1982b) describes needs as those things that motivate us when we get them and distress us when we do not. Each personality type has different needs. These needs are listed here and described in further detail as we look more deeply at each personality type below.

- Feelers need *acceptance of self* and *sensory satisfaction*.
- Thinkers need *recognition for work* and *time structure*.
- Believers need *recognition for work* and *conviction*.
- Dreamers need *solitude*.
- Funsters need *playful contact*.
- Doers need *incidence* (short-term activities with quick payoffs).

### Phases

The base is the strongest part of one's personality structure; those strongest aspects of each person are evident by six months of age (Kahler and Capers 1974; Kahler 1995a). One's phase describes where each of us finds positive motivation by getting our needs met. This may be described by the personality type of our base or elsewhere in our structure.

Individuals may experience a change in *phase* and move into another part of their structure. This means that they assume the predominant characteristics and, most importantly, the psychological needs (motivators) of that personality type under normal circumstances. Two-thirds of individuals will change their phase at least once during their lives. The dynamics that cause this change may be with or without our awareness. Phases last from two years to a lifetime and occur when individuals confront and *resolve* long-term, intense distress with a particular life issue. These issues (Kahler 1996d) are:

|            |                 |
|------------|-----------------|
| Feelers:   | anger           |
| Thinkers:  | grief           |
| Believers: | fear            |
| Dreamers:  | self-confidence |
| Funsters:  | self-love       |
| Doers:     | bonding         |

How these issues are interpreted into one's experience follows when each of the personality types is covered individually.

The person whose personality condominium is rendered in figure 3.2 is a Thinker (base) in a Believer phase. The strongest part of his (most likely, because 75 percent of Thinkers are male) personality involves seeing the world through thoughts, ideas, and logic. His current motivation comes from his Believer needs of *recognition of work* (as contributing in important ways) and *conviction*.

The probable reasons he phased (with or without his awareness) were because of resolving long-term distress first with grief (the issue for Thinkers) and then with anger (having *staged* through his Feeler). When he phased might not be pinpointed in time, but it is obvious that his preferences and motivation are different.

His friends and associates have probably noticed and commented how he seems more committed. He dresses differently—more according to the "rules" and less for comfort (as he might have dressed in his

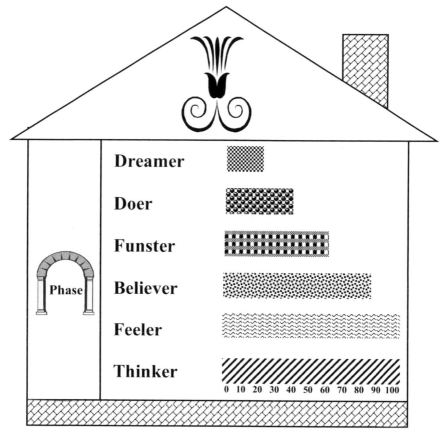

**Figure 3.2    Sample Phase Personality Condominium**

Feeler phase). He will interact more with regard for what others believe than for how they feel; however, results are still important to him.

Under normal circumstances, he will focus on what is wrong in slight distress (not getting the work recognition and conviction he *now* needs). If his needs continue to be unmet, he may preach or crusade and seem to attack others for their lack of commitment.

A Believer student of mine found himself overcommitted in terms of his job responsibilities, extracurricular activities, and the scheduling of his doctoral courses during one early summer. He wrote a long note to one of my colleagues berating us for not understanding how busy working students are at the end of the school year and how we had failed to apprise him of the summer schedule early enough. He went further to say that he would do all he could to get the schedule changed so future groups of students would be accommodated better.

His failure to plan carefully or manage his time better was overlooked in deference to our not "being perfect" and furthermore our not understanding our students' needs. These are both examples of the first- and second-degree distress for Believers: first, we were not OK because we were not perfect, and second, we were preached at for not being more considerate *and* the student was going to crusade for better conditions.

If the person shown in figure 3.2 experiences severe distress, he will retreat back to his strongest "floor," his base. Here, the distress will be seen in his attempts to regain control by not allowing others to do their part and his becoming critical about fairness, responsibility, finances, and so on—the signs of a Thinker trying to get recognition for his good work, albeit negatively.

The predictable nature of Process Communication is its value to understanding others. This understanding leads to effective communication.

## WHO ARE EDUCATORS?

Educators are predominantly (more than 85 percent) Believers, Feelers, and Thinkers in their base, beyond the broader distribution patterns (65 percent) in the general population cited above (Gilbert 1994). Notably conspicuous is the extremely limited number of any base Doers (less than 1 percent) and a very small percentage of phase Doers among educators. (A more complete discussion of the research is found in appendix B and arrayed in tables B.1 and B.2.)

The current *phases* of educators are also predominantly (more than 80 percent) Believers, Feelers, and Thinkers, with relatively few (less than 20 percent) people motivated extrinsically, as are Dreamers, Funsters, and Doers. So most educators see the world through *emotions, thoughts,* or *beliefs* and are motivated by *acceptance of themselves* as people or by *recognition for their work* (either as being done well or contributing to the purpose of the school or organization).

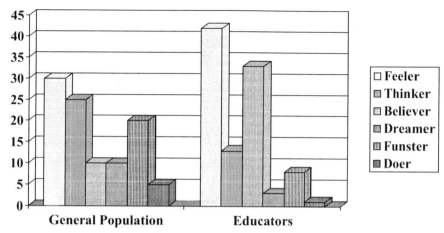

Figure 3.3   Distribution of Base Personalities

Students at risk tend not to be strong in the same characteristics of the educators (teachers and administrators) that work with them. They seem to cluster as Funsters and Doers. *Students with higher grade point averages (GPAs) tend to interact with the personality types most like their teachers* better than those whose performance is lower (Gilbert 1994; these data are found in appendix B). This supports the notion that grades are partially the ability of students to meet teacher expectations.

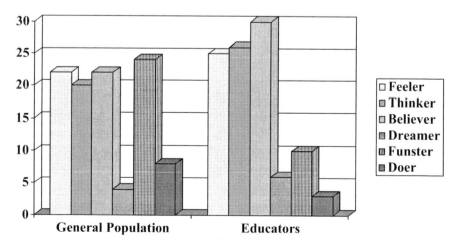

Figure 3.4   Distribution of Phase Personalities

Conversely, what this means is that those students who are at risk will probably be at greater risk when confronted by teachers weak in the energy needed to communicate with those student types effectively. Student grades are significantly affected by students' base personalities (Wallin 1993). Teachers trained in Process Communication have been shown to have a positive impact on student achievement (Hawking 1995).

Educators typically have high levels of energy to interact with Feelers, Thinkers, and Believers—those most like themselves. They also have a commensurately low amount of energy to interact with Dreamers, Funsters, and Doers. What this means in practical terms is that those people who are most like them will thrive, and those least like them will flounder. (An extensive examination of the classroom uses of Process Communication can be found in *Here's How to Reach Me* [Pauley, Bradley, and Pauley 2002].)

It is important to note that people must have sufficient energy to communicate with people whose personalities are markedly different from theirs. That is, if the "furnishings" on the upper floors of our condominiums are sparse, staying on those floors for long periods of time is likely to be uncomfortable and will cause us to go to where we have more to work with, more furnishing, more energy. Also, unless we get our needs met regularly (and positively), we are not likely going to be able to get in our "elevators" and go to those less-furnished floors; moreover, we are not likely to even want to "call" the elevator.

## INTERACTION STYLES

We interact with others according to how we prefer others to interact with us. Each personality type shows the preferences of interacting autocratically, democratically, benevolently, or in a laissez-faire manner (Kahler 1982a). These behaviors are typical, predictable, and habitual. Choosing another style requires that the effective leader move to another's *frame of preference.*

Because of their predominance either to be Feelers, Believers, or Thinkers, educators will also prefer either *benevolent* or *democratic* interaction (administrative) styles. That is, the way that they choose to relate to others will be either caring and person oriented or will be task oriented and designed to invite the participation of others in activities or decisions. Those with whom they have the most difficulty communicating will prefer either an *autocratic* (directive) or *laissez-faire* (nondirective) style. Neither of these styles is strong for most educators. These interaction preferences are listed in table 3.2 (from Kahler [1982a] adapted with permission).

## DAY-TO-DAY OPERATIONS

Students and teachers are quite capable, under *positive* conditions, of using the behaviors and preferences of more than one of the personality types. So the teacher can offer a lesson appropriate for Feelers—group activities—and have most students succeed. (Note that neither the teacher nor the students need to be base Feelers for this to happen.)

But what if the teacher offers instruction in only one mode? We can predict with certainty which students will lose energy and begin their failure patterns. PCM is very precise; we can anticipate the actual behaviors of a particular type of student *before* he or she fails. Using this

**Table 3.2   Interaction Styles**

| Interaction Style | Characteristics | Advantages | Disadvantages |
|---|---|---|---|
| Autocratic | Commands; directives; direct responses | Useful for those who require direction or structure | Does not invite group interaction or upward feedback |
| Democratic | Group participation; interaction between/ among others | Encourages self-paced growth; increases group cohesion; enhances morale | Does not provide enough structure for those who need it, or who lack knowledge and understanding |
| Benevolent | Belonging; caring; nurturing; accepting | Works well with those who need unconditional acceptance | Possibly seen as invasion of privacy, or personal trespass on professional relationships |
| Laissez-Faire | Nondirective | Works well for self-styled people, inviting independence and creativity | Does not provide direction and structure |

information, the teacher can intervene early and invite students back into their success patterns. What makes this work is that students prefer to succeed and will cooperate with a teacher who appears to understand them, accept them, and accommodate their learning preferences sincerely.

A somewhat exaggerated example of an application of the PCM is taken from the mathematics curriculum—the workbook. At the top of the page are usually a sample problem and a brief explanation of the concept. This is followed by twenty or so similar problems. One page is assigned each day, five days a week, for the six-week unit. Students are to work alone, not talk to their neighbors, and raise their hands for teacher help. If the work is particularly hard, confusing, or boring, we can make some predictions.

- Thinkers and Believers will be irritated but work hard to figure out the problems.
- Funsters will be confused, act out, and perhaps drop their books or fall out of their chairs.
- Doers will take some action to have the rules changed for them; they may try to make a deal with the teacher or just not do the work.
- Feelers will feel bad not having personal contact with others and may make silly mistakes. Initially, they may smile at their mistakes, but eventually they may cry (especially if they are younger students).
- Dreamers would have the best chance of succeeding, as this would present a set way of doing assignments that does not involve interacting with the teacher or other students. If they cannot do the work, they will wait passively for the end of the period.

Staying with the context of mathematics instruction, here is a positive example of how to meet the needs of all of the student types. (Thanks to Roxanne Lee, a PCM-trained teacher in Sheridan, Arkansas.) The exemplary activity was to determine rate of speed by applying the component variables of distance and time. The class was divided into groups of two to four students. Each group had a battery-powered car and a stopwatch. Their task was to name their car, run it over a fifteen-foot course, and take the average of five runs. Each group's average was then used to predict which car would win a twenty-five-foot race and what the order of finish would be. Finally, the race was run, and the results were compared to the predictions.

- Thinkers and Believers were interested in the *structure* of the race-course, the *data*, and the *rules* of the activity.
- Funsters *liked* the group nature of this *fun* activity, especially the *creative* naming of the car and the opportunity to *play* with their buddies.
- Doers were energized by the *incidence* (number of activities).
- Feelers *enjoyed* being with a group and wanted everyone to *feel good* about what they were doing.
- Dreamers functioned best as data recorders, being *left alone* to do their part.

All students had an integral part in the lesson and did not experience the distress of not having their needs met. Although this is a useful example of how to keep students *on task*, not all lessons or instructional units will have a full range of activities. When the lessons are more singular in their approach, educators will need to assist others in getting their needs met first and then invite them to access other, less-preferred aspects of their personalities.

The PCM is simple, yet comprehensive and thorough, covering interaction styles, channels of communication, psychological needs, physical environments, perceptions of the environment, driver behaviors, failure patterns, and failure mechanisms. At first blush, the model may appear difficult to understand because of its comprehensiveness. However, successful teachers and administrators find they are already using some of the information, and they can add new strategies one piece at a time. The best news is that it works, providing ways for all people to succeed and remain positive.

## OUTCOMES

As mentioned, many *at-risk* students are either Doers or Funsters. For Thinker, Feeler, or Believer educators (the predominant types), communicating with Doers and Funsters requires more energy than with the other personality types; thus, many students might have unmet needs and experience the normal distress or severe distress that accompanies this lack of fulfillment. With Thinker as the least-developed personality type of these at-risk students, traditional (highly structured, with much "drill-and-skill" seatwork, etc.) programs designed to "help" students organize their work better or think more logically are destined to fail. Such approaches appeal to Thinker types and, therefore, fare no better with at-risk students than trying to extinguish a fire with gasoline, often with equally inflamed results for both the teacher and student.

An example of the profound effects that Process Communication can have was found in the Apache Junction (Arizona) School District. Officials of that district chose to upgrade their professional staff in interpersonal skills and classroom control. *Every* professional staff member attended at least a three-day session on Process Communication. During these three-day sessions, participants explored PCM, identified what their base personality and personality sequence were, how to energize themselves, and learned how to arrange to get their psychological needs met daily, weekly, and monthly. They also learned how to interact effectively and motivate each student type, how to interpret negative behaviors in students and intervene quickly and effectively, and how to monitor their distress signals and take appropriate, positive action.

The following *one-year* results were attributed by school officials to the study and use of PCM:

- *Employee turnover* had been reduced from 43 percent to less than 3 percent (even with lower salaries than in neighboring districts—reinforcing the argument that salary is not the primary determinant of attracting and retaining staff);
- *Employee satisfaction* and staff morale reached an all-time high;
- *Student achievement* at every grade level increased dramatically;
- The *failure rate* in grades 7 and 8 *decreased* from 20 percent to less than 2 percent;
- *Disciplinary referrals* were reduced to less than 2 percent on any given day;
- The *dropout rate* declined from more than 20 percent to less than 9 percent;

- *Graduation* rates increased;
- Students entering *postsecondary training* increased from less than 19 percent to more than 43 percent; and
- The *satisfaction* of parents and students toward the schooling process improved substantially. (Gilbert 1992)

These results suggest strongly that meeting the communication needs of individuals can play an integral part in school improvement. The outcomes in Apache Junction were so compelling that the district extended the training to include all support personnel as well as professional staff. Further, the superintendent was named superintendent of the year in Arizona, an honor he attributed to the success of Process Communication in his district.

## BENEFITS OF PCM

It is important to understand that the PCM focuses on *process*—not content—and process is a more challenging focus and takes longer to change. The exciting result is that changing process can relate to all aspects of the school organization that involve communication. The benefits are both tangible and intangible. The most tangible benefit is that students attend better and stay in school—of course, this translates into more dollars if revenue is based on some function of attendance. The greatest intangible benefit is more effective communication throughout the organization—administrators and staff, staff and students, and staff with each other. Moreover, this benefit carries over into the home, where communication becomes more effective between the participants and their families.

In addition, the implementation of Process Communication may give people in conflict an opportunity to move away from adversarial negotiations into "nonadversarial bargaining," which fosters consensus building and mutually acceptable decisions. This approach can yield a decision in a short meeting, made by and supported by the participating parties.

## CONCLUSION

Changing the processes that we use in education is more difficult and takes longer than changing what we know—and that might not be effective. Many educators subscribe to the notion that students and staff must function within specific (singular) behavior patterns in order for them to succeed. This limited perspective ignores the diversity of needs we confront as educators. We need to take the time and find sufficient energy to deal effectively with the differences that confront us. Understanding ourselves and others, knowing what negative behaviors mean and what to do about them in the school setting, while focusing more and more on *how* we communicate, can have profound positive consequences in education.

## POINTS TO PONDER

- People are comprised of varying characteristics of six personality types.
- The aspects of the predominant personalities determine how individuals behave.

**Table 3.3   Who Am I?**

With all of the information presented in this chapter, you might be wondering who you are—that is, what are your communication characteristics and preferences?

| If you see the world through . . . | And if you are energized by . . . | You have strong tendencies to be a |
| --- | --- | --- |
| Thoughts and ideas | Recognition for work and time structure | *Thinker* |
| Feelings and emotions | Acceptance of who you are and sensory satisfaction | *Feeler* |
| Beliefs, values, and opinions | Recognition of your valuable work and conviction | *Believer* |
| Reflections and imagination | Being alone and solitary | *Dreamer* |
| Likes and dislikes | Playful contact | *Funster* |
| Actions | Lots of activities in short bursts with quick payoffs | *Doer* |

- The base personality describes the strongest tendencies of a person, especially perceptual preferences.
- The phase personality describes how people are motivated—what they need.
- People generally try to get their needs met positively.
- When they do not get their needs met positively, they will attempt to get the same needs met negatively in very predictable ways seen in varying levels of distress.
- People communicate easiest with those who are similar to them. Those who are very different present greater challenges.
- Effective communication occurs when a message is offered and accepted using an appropriate channel.

## REFERENCES

Berne, E. 1964. *Games people play: The psychology of human relationships.* New York: Grove Press.

De Bono, E. 1985. *Six thinking hats.* Toronto: Little, Brown and Co.

Gardner, H. 1983. *Frames of mind: The theory of multiple intelligences.* New York: Basic Books.

Gilbert, M. B. 1992. Dreamers, rebels, and others: Personality styles affect communication. *Executive Educator* (June): 32–33.

———. 1994. Meeting communication needs of students can promote success. Little Rock: University of Arkansas at Little Rock. (Unpublished report of Off-Campus Duty Assignment)

———.1997. An examination of the listening effectiveness of educators: Performance versus preference. Presentation at the annual convention of the International Listening Association, March, Mobile, Ala.

Gregorc, A. 1982. *Gregorc style delineator.* Maynard, Mass.: Gabriel Systems.

Hawking N. G. 1995. A study of the impact on student achievement by teachers trained in process communication. Unpublished doctoral diss., University of Arkansas at Little Rock.

Johnson, D. W. 1993. *Reaching out: Interpersonal effectiveness and self-actualization.* 5th ed. Englewood Cliffs, N.J.: Prentice-Hall.

Kahler, T. 1979. *Process therapy in brief.* Little Rock, Ark.: Human Development Publications.

———. 1982a. *Personality pattern inventory validation studies.* Little Rock, Ark.: Kahler Communications.

———. 1982b. *Process communication model: A contemporary model for organizational development.* Little Rock, Ark.: Kahler Communications.

———. 1992. *The process communication management seminar.* Little Rock, Ark.: Kahler Communications.

———. 1995a. A brief: Passing through. *Transactional Analysis Journal* 25 (1): 57.

———. 1995b. *The process teaching seminar.* Little Rock, Ark.: Kahler Communications.

———. 1996a. *Personality pattern inventory.* Little Rock, Ark.: Kahler Communications.

———. 1996b. *The key to me for students profile.* Little Rock, Ark.: Kahler Communications.

———. 1996c. *The key to me for educators profile.* Little Rock, Ark.: Kahler Communications.

———. 1996d. *The key to me seminar.* Little Rock, Ark.: Kahler Communications.

———. 2000. *The mastery of management.* Little Rock, Ark.: Kahler Communications.

Kahler, T., and H. Capers. 1974. The miniscript. *Transactional Analysis Journal* 4 (1): 26–42.

Keirsey, D., and M. Bates. 1984. *Please understand me: Character and temperament types.* Del Mar, Calif.: Prometheus Nemesis Books.

Kolb, D. A. 1984. *Experiential learning: Experience as the source of learning and development.* Englewood Cliffs, N.J.: Prentice-Hall.

Maslow, A. H. 1954. *Motivation and personality.* New York: Harper.

McCarthy, B. 1980. *The 4MAT system: Teaching to learning styles with right/left mode techniques.* Barrington, Ill.: Excel.

Myers, I. B., and K. C. Briggs. (1943, 1976, 1985). *Myers-Briggs type indicator.* Palo Alto, Calif.: Consulting Psychologists Press.

Noland, J. R. 1978. *Personalysis.* St. Paul, Minn.: Communication Development.

Pauley, J. A., D. F. Bradley, and J. F. Pauley. 2002. *Here's how to reach me: Matching instruction to personality types in the classroom.* Baltimore, Md.: Paul H. Brookes Publishing.

Wallin, M. B. 1993. "Making" the grade: The effects of teacher personality types on student grading practices. *Dissertation Abstracts International* 53 (11): 3854. University Microfilms no. AAT9307147.

# Section II

# PERSONALITY BUILDING BLOCKS: ATTRIBUTES AND PROBLEM SITUATIONS

## WHAT'S TO COME

This section describes six *pure* personality types, recognizing that no one is singular but a composite of each of these personalities in varying degrees. Each person will be seen in both positive and negative ways, all of which are predictable.

*To emphasize*: you will never meet any of the people exactly as they are described below. What you will encounter are people who will show you aspects of the preferences and behaviors of one of the six people you are about to meet. In the real world, you may notice that people change. When this occurs, you will see another aspect of who they are, but they are still the same people.

Following the narrative description of each person will be a profile including the following components:

- Character Strengths
- Perceptual Preference
- Communication Channel
- Psychological Needs
- Administrative Style
- Driver

- Failure Mechanism
- Distress Mask
- Life Issue

## PURE EDUCATOR PERSONALITIES

Each of our six educators—Barbara, Alfred, Matthew, Dorothy, Angie, and Doug—is presented as a *pure* personality type. You will see each person as if there are no components of other personalities. As you understand the unique characteristics of each person, you will begin to see the different aspects of personalities that are *combined* in each of us in varying degrees of strength. Please note that we are combinations of all of these personalities. We have preferences for communicating and the ability to shift to other positions when invited and if we are OK ourselves.

You will speculate about yourself—wondering what your base is, and in what phase you are currently. The description of each person will give you good hints about yourself. The purpose is that you be able to understand others as you interact with them in your professional and personal life. (See also table 3.3, "Who Am I?" in chapter 3.)

## PROBLEMS SITUATIONS AND
## SUGGESTIONS FOR RESOLUTION

Following your introduction to each personality, you will be presented with problem situations that demonstrate the *predictable* distress of each personality type, or situations that may foster distress if not handled deftly. You will encounter a key actor showing negative behaviors or presenting an important perspective for you to ponder. These behaviors indicate that the individual lacks positive motivation—that is, his or her needs are not being met positively. *Symptoms for Consideration* will be offered, followed by *Suggestions for Action*.

# FOUR

## Pure Feeler: Barbara

Barbara ("Bobbie" to her numerous friends) is a *compassionate, sensitive,* and *warm* person. She's a Feeler—a very giving person. Her parents marveled at her warmth and caring nature from the time she was quite young. She decided to become an educator because she wanted to help others become healthy people emotionally and to be able to help others themselves to prepare for life. Barbara's life is filled with sensual things. Her home is warm and inviting. It is decorated to appeal to the senses—potpourri, flowers and other fragrant things, soft and comfortable places to sit, and earth-tone colors throughout. Her office has reminders of the precious and familiar things in her life—photographs of the family (including her special friend, Ernie, a cat she named after her favorite Sesame Street character), soft petit-point pillows, and a wall hanging her father got on a trip to Africa.

She sees the world through her emotions. She wants to know how others feel and that they are OK. "How do you *feel?*" is a question she is likely to ask, and she will be very attentive to the answer. She is most comfortable when she can interact with others—individually or in groups. She prefers to have people around her and work closely with them. She is motivated intrinsically but almost always with a thought of what she perceives others may need. Barbara is likely to offer and give (and receive) hugs often. She may touch others when talking with them, especially if she knows her touch is welcome. *Warm fuzzies*, things that invite people to feel good, are her preference—to give and receive.

Barbara needs *acceptance of self* and *sensory satisfaction*. She needs to know she is appreciated and wanted, and she takes advantage of opportunities to experience things that appeal to her senses. She can never be around too many people. At social gatherings, she would be sure everyone were comfortable, fed, and in a "good place," even if she were not hosting the gathering. You might find her in the kitchen, serving food or drink, or being sure that everyone has been introduced to everyone else.

She will try to help those who are having any type of difficulty—from fixing a balky zipper to smoothing out a stormy relationship. She is highly empathic—to the point of mirroring someone else's emotions or what he "should" be feeling. She is in her element if she can provide support or aid to others.

Barbara will dress in comfortable and visually pleasing clothes. The fabrics she chooses will feel good to the touch, especially hers. Her hair will be arranged nicely and with care. She will wear her favorite fragrances. If she has only one favorite, it will be her "signature smell."

She prefers to work with people who accept her unconditionally—either as a teacher or administrator. At the elementary level, she would work well with primary children; in high school, she would likely teach life skills (what may have been called "home economics" formerly). As an administrator, it would be important to Barbara to work in a people-oriented situation. Besides being a school-site administrator, she might choose to be a counselor or perhaps director of personnel. Working in a position that was highly task oriented without much personal contact would weaken her emotionally. (She would be the archetypal 1,9 manager, using the Blake and Mouton Managerial Grid [1985]. She would show a very high degree of concern for people and a commensurately low degree of concern for production.)

Barbara is likely to remark about how pleasant someone else looks or smells. She will focus almost exclusively on the positives of other people and is unlikely to criticize them face-to-face. However, she might ask a colleague if something is wrong with someone she senses is having difficulty—at home or at work. She will want to know if there is something she can do "to make it better." While her own needs are important, sometimes she will set them aside when she *feels* someone else *needs* her.

She is prone to using "smiley faces" and flowery handwriting, and is very attentive to others. She is likely to bring home-baked cookies or muffins to the faculty lounge or to staff meetings. Most of her actions are meant to "make" others feel good.

(The perception of "making others feel good" is one of the *myths* of interaction [Kahler 1978]. We cannot force others to feel a certain way, nor can others control how we feel. We have a choice; however, certain things in our environment may be very compelling for how we choose to feel. For example, when confronted with sad stories, Feelers may also *feel* sad; others may not.)

Barbara's predominant administrative style is *benevolent*. She will work with others in a way designed for them to be comfortable and welcome. She is person oriented and focuses more on people than thoughts or tasks. The feelings of others are most important to her. Her presumption is that when people "feel" good, they perform better and interact more effectively. Her style is to foster a sense of belonging in others by interacting with them in nurturing and accepting ways.

She will communicate predominantly through a *nurturative* channel. Her words, tones, gestures, posture, and facial expressions are caring and warm. She will attempt to comfort others as a nurturing parent would. She wants them to know that "I really appreciate you, and I look forward to being with you. I want to help you feel good."

If she has an unfinished issue in life, it is likely to be *anger*. Her need for acceptance of herself and to accept others overrides giving herself permission to be angry. This difficulty with being angry or expressing anger in appropriate ways is likely to be distressful for her: "If I express my anger at you, I will have hurt your feelings and/or you will reject me. Therefore, I will please you and hold in my anger" (Kahler 1996a).

If Barbara is unable to get her *acceptance of self* or *sensory satisfaction* needs met positively, she will begin to show predictable driver (the first indicator of distress) behaviors by overadapting in an attempt to *please* others. (Distress behaviors or patterns are an attempt to get the same needs met *negatively*.) She is moving into an "I'm not OK—you're OK" position. She will show this posture with or without her awareness. She will overadapt to situations or people: "Could you . . . maybe . . . take, sorta, a careful look at this?"

If the *please you* driver does not allow Barbara to attain what she needs (and it usually does not), she will don a *Drooper* mask and, again predictably, slip into second-degree distress. Here she will feel sad, worried, anxious, or confused. She will give off *warning signals* of lacking assertiveness, laughing at herself, or acting "stupid." It may seem as if she is wearing a "Kick me!" sign. If her needs are not met over time, she may look different. She may not be as careful in her dress or appearance as she is usually. She may even appear depressed. If her distress continues for a long period, she may even become hysterical at times.

Her *failure mechanism* is making mistakes, which is *not* related to her intelligence or her competence. These warning signs suggest that Barbara is not motivated positively. *She* needs to arrange to be nurtured unconditionally either by herself or a warm and caring person in her life—someone who will let her know she is important to him or her and who will listen to how she feels. Barbara also needs to nurture herself sensually—with a bubble bath, new clothes, or spending time with people who like her for herself and have no ulterior motives.

If Barbara works with a supervisor who does not understand her *needs,* she is likely to request a transfer to a more nurturing environment or she may seek employment elsewhere. These potential alternatives may not be true options, because Barbara is likely to be highly place-bound. That is, she is not likely to pick up and move easily. She may be a secondary wage earner in her household, or she may be inextricably tied to her location/environment with a large circle of family and friends. As a result, she may stay in distress and be less productive in both her professional and personal lives.

## BARBARA'S PROFILE

| | |
|---|---|
| Character Strengths: | Compassionate, sensitive, warm |
| Perceptual Preference: | Emotions |
| Communication Channel: | Nurturative |
| Psychological Needs: | Acceptance of self; sensory satisfaction |
| Administrative Style: | Benevolent |
| Driver: | Please you |
| Failure Mechanism: | Makes mistakes; invites criticism |
| Distress Mask: | Drooper |
| Life Issue: | Anger |

(Adapted with permission from Kahler [1995, 1996b].)

## PROBLEM SITUATION

Barbara has been a teacher in your school for twelve years. Of late, you have noticed that she is often late, appears slovenly, and turns in sloppy and inaccurate reports. Her enthusiasm for teaching and her caring for her students also seem to have diminished. These behaviors are different from what she has shown previously. You have heard that she is having some difficulty at home. As her principal, you are concerned.

### Symptoms for Consideration

Barbara has changed her behavior dramatically. Her *appearance* and the *mistakes* she is making indicates she may be in Feeler distress. She has not arranged to have her *acceptance of self* and *sensory* needs met—apparently both at home and at work. She has probably shown a lot of "please you" behaviors by attempting to overadapt to people and situations, and has been unsuccessful in getting her needs met through accommodating others. She is inviting criticism in her negative posture and has assumed a "Kick me!" stance.

### Suggestions for Action

- Tell her how pleased you are to see her each day. Let her know that her presence brightens the lives of children and adds to organization.
- Ask her how her family is. Listen to her empathically if she chooses to "unload" with you about any problems she may be having at home. (Note: Be sure you have the time to offer her, or set up some time for her to talk with you. This may be accomplished best at the end of the day, in case her catharsis leaves her emotionally drained.)
- Appreciate *her* publicly at a faculty meeting. (Note: As you express your appreciation of her, focus on her as a person, not on what she has accomplished. For example, say "Barbara is one of the most caring people I know. The school family means a great deal to her.")
- Support her unconditionally, even though she may be having prob-

lems. Invite her to take some days off to do something to pamper herself, thereby regaining the necessary energy to move her from her distress.

- If you do not perceive it as favoritism, give her a small gift that indicates you appreciate her—a "big hug mug," a package of pot-pourri, or something else that will appeal to her senses. (Male administrators may want to consider if these small pieces of appreciation may be perceived as inappropriate, given current concerns of sexual harassment.)

(Adapted with permission from Kahler [1982, 1995].)

## REFERENCES

Blake, R. R., and J. S. Mouton. 1985. *The managerial grid III: A new look at the classic that has boosted productivity and profits for thousands of corporations worldwide*. Houston: Gulf Publishing.

Kahler, T. 1978. *TA revisited*. Little Rock, Ark.: Human Development Publications.

———. 1982. *Personality pattern inventory studies*. Little Rock, Ark.: Kahler Communications.

———. 1995. *The process teaching seminar*. Little Rock, Ark.: Kahler Communications.

———. 1996a. *The advanced process communication seminar*. Little Rock, Ark.: Kahler Communications.

———. 1996b. *The key to me seminar*. Little Rock, Ark.: Kahler Communications.

# FIVE

## Pure Thinker: Alfred

Alfred is a *logical, responsible,* and *organized* person. He decided to become an educator because he recognized his strong ability to organize learning activities, to put concepts into logical sequences, and to offer instruction in a timely and focused fashion. His life is structured into sensible and time-oriented blocks. His home is highly functional—everything in its place and a place for everything.

His office is arranged for efficiency. His desk is orderly and usually clean and uncluttered at the end of each day. His workspace is designed so he can get to needed equipment and files easily. His computer is state-of-the-art, with a fast processor and a large amount of random-access memory (RAM) and file storage capacity (probably more than he will ever use, but one never knows). He has backup, security, and power-surge protection to prevent tampering and any kind of information loss. Alfred (never "Al") prefers to do things only once. His office has a large array of certificates, plaques, and awards, attesting to his accomplishments and hard work.

Alfred experiences the world through his thoughts, ideas, and logic. He expects others to think clearly and be responsible for themselves and for their work. He does not "suffer fools easily." He prefers to work alone or one-on-one. He is motivated intrinsically—that is, he does not need to be stimulated or motivated much by others.

When he asks a question, he expects a direct answer—one that responds to what he asked. When working with others, he wants them to be prepared. He is impressed by independent thinking, but only if the basic material has been learned first.

As a teacher, Alfred would work best in structured subjects—mathematics, physical science, and so on—areas that are highly predictable and that have logical boundaries. As an administrator, he is likely to focus on order—in people and things. Rules are established for order. Discipline and orderly procedures would be paramount in any venture he might oversee. His reports would be neat, precise, and on time. He would not need to make all the decisions, but he would insist that decisions be made rationally and sensibly.

Alfred needs *recognition for work* and *time structure*. He wants to know that others acknowledge his hard work and clear thinking. His life, both personal and professional, is orderly and timely. He can "play" but only if he has finished his work first. The "games" he chooses usually have clear rules and outcomes. He is likely to gravitate to those things that are precise—chess, checkers, bridge, knowledge/trivia games, and so forth. He has difficulty with amorphous things—before he starts, he wants to be sure he knows the objective and will move definitively in that direction. He maps his routes before he begins—whether he is traveling or planning for organizational change. His schedule tends not to be overbooked, insofar as he can schedule all he has to do. Unscheduled intrusions are bothersome; he prefers people to make appointments (and keep them). He does "schedule" unencumbered time to be out and about—managing by wandering around (Peters and Austin 1985).

Arriving at work at approximately the same time and before things become too busy, Alfred gets into each day in predictable fashion—returning phone calls, checking his electronic and postal mail, working with his secretary on correspondence and other areas, and similar duties. He understands that school things are not always orderly and structured, so he does what he can to control those things he can. He works best when things go as planned.

Alfred will acknowledge a job well done. He would focus on the degree of accomplishment and the precision or accuracy of the work. For things done particularly well, he might send a letter or a certificate. He would use plaques or trophies for noteworthy outcomes and present them at a formal assembly. He is not likely to be effusive in rewarding things done well, but he will be sure that others understand the importance of working hard and well. (As Barbara would manage in the 1,9

Blake-Mouton style, Alfred would be a very strong 9,1 manager, with a high degree of concern for completed tasks and a low degree of concern for people. His focus would be on the work.)

Being *democratic* is Alfred's predominant administrative style. He subscribes strongly to principles of group participation in decision making in the proper context. He will encourage interaction between and among others, solicit feedback, and foster independent thinking. He thinks this style will encourage goal-oriented people to grow at their own pace, will increase group cohesion, and will enhance morale because of a focus on common goals (Kahler 1982a).

Alfred will use a *requestive* channel to communicate with others and prefers it be used with him. His main objective in communicating with others is the receiving and sharing of information, usually related to getting the work done: "What do you think our options are?"

If Alfred has a life issue to resolve, it is likely to be *grief*. He may experience long-term intense distress with a focus on what might be lost if clear thinking and predictable schedules are not the order of the day—"If I don't do the thinking for you, then something bad will happen. Therefore, I will be perfect and not make any mistakes . . . and as long as I am critical or you're not thinking clearly, I can avoid my grief" (Kahler 1996a).

If Alfred is not able to get his *recognition for work* and *time structure* needs met positively, he will show the predictable *"be perfect"* driver behaviors—pulling back on delegation of tasks and taking on more work for himself: *"If I work harder and longer, then people will recognize my good work."* He may make an overqualified statement as an indicator of his distress: *"I am not exactly, precisely sure that is the option we should consider."* If his distress (lack of needs fulfillment) continues, he will don an *Attacker* mask and attempt to overcontrol others. The warning signs are his being easily frustrated with those who do not think the same or clearly, and becoming fussy with ("attacking") others around issues of money, order, and responsibility.

This "attacking" is likely to spill over into his personal life with his spouse and his children. He will have difficulty understanding how people can get through life without clear thinking, how irrational or nonrational behavior can be acceptable, or why others do not or cannot see the logic of how things can go smoothly if being responsible and thinking clearly guide your actions. The more Alfred stays in distress, the longer he will work—foregoing recreation, vacations, retirement. His absence from others who need his presence may cause them distress (especially if he is married to the caring Feeler). He thinks he is working for them, and does not realize that he is trying to get his own needs met by working longer and harder—not being recognized for his work.

If Alfred works with a supervisor who does not understand his *needs*, he is likely to do "battle" around thinking issues—not thinking clearly, making "silly" mistakes, being irresponsible. However, it would be unusual for Alfred to be supervised in education by someone who did not recognize his work, detail, or structure. His distress might come from disagreement with his ideas or failure to focus on issues needing to be addressed.

## ALFRED'S PROFILE

| | |
|---|---|
| Character Strengths: | Logical, responsible, organized |
| Perceptual Preference: | Thoughts |
| Communication Channel: | Requestive |
| Psychological Needs: | Recognition for work; time structure |
| Administrative Style: | Democratic |
| Driver: | Be perfect |
| Failure Mechanism: | Overcontrols |
| Distress Mask: | Attacker |
| Life Issue: | Grief |

(Adapted with permission from Kahler [1995, 1996b].)

## PROBLEM SITUATION

Alfred is a curriculum specialist who has been on the job for twelve years and who is retiring at year's end. He has begun to take it upon himself to criticize members of the school staff about their performance of their job responsibilities, even though he serves in a staff capacity with no supervisory responsibilities. He had been given more and more authority for discretionary action for curricular affairs over the years, leading to a somewhat intimidating demeanor, especially for the newer staff members. He is critical about punctuality (both for arrival at school and for assignments and reports), how cocurricular and extracurricular activities are supervised (especially with reports of monies collected), the way in which materials and supplies are requested by the staff, and other similar instances.

### Symptoms for Consideration

Alfred is demonstrating Thinker distress—picky about details and time. He expects others to think clearly so that things will go smoothly. If they do not, he will take on more and more, because only he knows how to do what needs to be done—and he can do "it" faster and more efficiently.

His distress is occasioned by his not getting his Thinker needs met—*recognition for work* and *time structure*. To motivate him, you, as his supervisor, will consider how to move from negative to positive needs satisfaction.

### Suggestions for Action

- Intervene into his distress by acknowledging that he is working well (if, indeed, he is): "Good job!" "You work very efficiently." "Your ideas about how to get things done are very sensible."
- Write him a note acknowledging his work, or present him with a Certificate of Accomplishment.
- Give him thoughtful problems to solve that relate to his areas of responsibility—"Can you suggest how we might rethink distributing supplies?"
- Let him know time frames for projects as he is assigned them, or ask him how long it will take him to complete a task.

(Adapted with permission from Kahler [1982b, 1995].)

### REFERENCES

Blake, R. R., and J. S. Mouton. 1985. *The managerial grid III: A new look at the classic that has boosted productivity and profits for thousands of corporations worldwide.* Houston: Gulf Publishing.

Kahler, T. 1982a. *Process communication model: A contemporary model for organizational development.* Little Rock, Ark.: Kahler Communications.

———. 1982b. *Personality pattern inventory studies.* Little Rock, Ark.: Kahler Communications.

———. 1995. *The process teaching seminar.* Little Rock, Ark.: Kahler Communications.

———. 1996a. *The advanced process communication seminar.* Little Rock, Ark.: Kahler Communications.

———. 1996b. *The key to me seminar.* Little Rock, Ark.: Kahler Communications.

Peters, T., and N. Austin. 1985. *A passion for excellence: The leadership difference.* New York: Random House.

# SIX

## Pure Believer: Matthew

Matthew is a *conscientious, dedicated,* and *observant* person. He decided to become an educator because he recognized what is important and valuable for people to learn so that they can become productive members of society. His life focuses on things that support his beliefs and values. He is very interested in politics, religion, and current events. His home is arrayed with books, pictures, and sayings that relate to his belief system. He believes his name shows the strength of his convictions and prefers to be called "Matthew," rather than the shortened "Matt."

Matthew experiences the world through his beliefs and opinions. He gravitates toward people, issues, and situations that affirm his values. As with Alfred, Matthew prefers to work alone or one-on-one. When he asks a question, he expects a direct answer—one that responds to what he asked. When working with others, he wants them to know what they are doing, but even more, he wants them to understand the importance of what they are doing—both for the current situation and for the long term. He will discuss issues and will listen to opposing points of view, accepting them only if his position has been accepted. On issues presented in a forum in which he is an observer—such as the newspaper—he is likely to offer an opposing point of view (e.g., letter to the editor) on a topic of deep concern to him. His zeal for causes and ideas important to him (usually politics, religion, or current events) is admirable—but can occasionally get in the way if he does not get his needs met.

As a teacher, Matthew might gravitate to social studies or literature, areas where he would be able to air his position and opinions and structure his lessons around them. He would focus on the importance of concepts and how they contribute to the overall scheme of things. For example, he might spend a lot of time on the "no-taxation-without-representation" notion that underlaid the Boston Tea Party. He would expect students to respect his belief system—and might show favoritism for those who did or respond negatively to those who did not.

His approach to discipline would be to do what is right, in an orderly way, and because "society" could not function without rules of behavior. He needs *recognition for work* and *conviction*. That is, he needs to have affirmed that his work is important and that others respect his belief system. He, too, can "play" but only if he has finished his work first. The rules of "life" must be observed before "frivolous" things can be done or "allowed." He is his own taskmaster and may become impatient if others direct him. He would prefer to be asked to take on an assignment or do a task.

Like Alfred, he finds his motivation from within, but he might also be motivated more readily by people or issues related to his belief system. He approaches his job with a sense of what is important to the mission of the organization. For example, he might choose to work on a grant proposal for a new curriculum strategy rather than complete a periodic intradistrict report. The report would be completed on time, but Matthew would see it as part of "administrivia," the busy work to be done. He acknowledges that some people "color outside the lines," but his position is that "lines" are there for a purpose.

He dresses as he believes one ought, given his position and rank in the organization. He does not insist that others dress similarly, but approaches those who do so more approvingly. Students who are untidy or who dress in a way he considers to be "careless" will get at least a mental "tsk tsk" from him.

As a leader, Matthew will not go overboard in recognizing good work because it is "what people *ought* to do." For exceptional merit, he would make a public acclamation of the valuable service of the individual and present the person with a framed print of one of his favorite sayings or a book subscribing to his beliefs.

Like Alfred, Matthew's preferred administrative style is *democratic*. He believes that staff members involved in decisions, especially those they have to implement, ought to participate to some degree in the making of those decisions. At times, however, he may become parental on a "very important" decision and make the decision himself, even if there is benefit to involving others. He might justify that position by saying that others did not have enough information or experience. This rationalization might cover up a *fear* that the "wrong" approach might be advocated. (He, too, would tend to the 9,1 style, focusing more on the work, which he believes is more important than the person.)

Matthew prefers a *requestive* channel of communication. He usually seeks information in his interchanges with others. He may also ask for justification of a position he does not understand or, more likely, a position with which he disagrees, "Why do you believe we ought to do that?" He might become more parental with, "Do you mean to tell me . . .?" This might be his way of opening a conversation that will focus on why someone else's position is wrong and untenable—in his mind.

If Matthew has a life issue to resolve, it is likely to be *fear*. He may experience long-term intense distress with a focus on what might happen if strong values and the "right" beliefs are not guideposts for action—"If I don't make sure you believe the right way and do the right things, then something bad will happen. Therefore, I expect you to be perfect and not make any mistakes and, as long as I am preaching at you, I can avoid my own fears" (Kahler 1996a).

If he does not get his *recognition for work* or *conviction* needs met positively, he will assume a parental *be perfect* driver position—focusing on what was done wrong, instead of affirming what was done correctly. He may ask an overqualifying question: "What exactly, precisely do you mean by that?" If Matthew's distress continues, he will don an *Attacker* mask (like Alfred) and become crusading or "preachy." The warning signals are either his being frustrated with those who do not believe as he does, or his being overly critical or suspicious of others.

This distress may carry over to his personal life. He may become picky with his spouse about the way the house looks or that small aspect of a meal that did not quite work. He will expect his children to excel and "fuss" at them for the incorrect (what he might interpret as "careless") responses on their homework or tests. He will go on and on about the value of an education and the importance of doing well. When he is in distress, no one in Matthew's life, including him, can escape his criti-

cism. His insistence that others *be perfect* can be damaging to his relationships, sometimes with dire consequences—divorce or children who
gravitate into dangerous situations, such as drugs or other behaviors that
are sure to garner their father's disapproval.

If Matthew works with a supervisor whose belief system is different
from his, he is likely to take that person to task on critical organizational
issues, even at the risk of his job. However, because educators tend to
be *based* in strong beliefs—more than three times the distribution in
the general population—Matthew is likely to find himself among colleagues who prefer to experience the world through their values and
opinions more often than not.

## MATTHEW'S PROFILE

Character Strengths:        Conscientious, dedicated, observant
Perceptual Preference:      Beliefs
Communication Channel:      Requestive
Psychological Needs:        Recognition for work; conviction
Administrative Style:       Democratic
Driver:                     You should be perfect
Failure Mechanism:          Crusades
Distress Mask:              Attacker
Life Issue:                 Fear

(Adapted with permission from Kahler [1995, 1996b].)

## PROBLEM SITUATION

Matthew, an experienced principal of an innovative and successful high
school, has approached you, as superintendent, with an idea to set up a
school-based health clinic to deal with some of the more pressing issues
he believes relate to his students. You had encouraged him to write a
proposal outlining the problems, a plan to address the problems, and a
budget. He has presented you with a plan to provide a number of different services, including the distribution of condoms, abortion counseling,

and similar activities. He has justified these services by citing the rising rates of sexually transmitted diseases and unwanted pregnancies. Because of the very sensitive nature of these issues and the negative impact this plan is likely to have on the school board and the community, you are inclined to reject the proposal.

### Symptoms for Consideration

Matthew has been encouraged to develop a sensitive project, one he *believes* is important. Whether or not you approve the project is inconsequential to keeping Matthew motivated and focused on the mission of the district. His strong *beliefs* indicate his Believer nature. He needs *acceptance of* these *convictions* and *recognition for* his *work*. (Note that acceptance of convictions does not mean you agree with him; only that you acknowledge his beliefs. Do not argue with him about whether his beliefs or opinions are right or wrong.) If you reject the project without ample explanation or justification, you are likely to see Matthew "preach" or "crusade" about the importance of dealing with such critical issues facing teenagers.

### Suggestions for Action

- Accept his proposal as it is written. Thank him for his hard work in developing a project so obviously important to him, and for believing in the welfare of the children. His having heard that, you may tell him that the way in which he has proposed dealing with the situation is not going to be approved by the board at this time (if that is your assessment). Invite him to raise the issue again at another time—be specific as to when you will be ready to consider it (six months, next year, etc.).
- Commend his overall work in a letter or with some public recognition (including sending on the acknowledgment to the appropriate media).
- Recognize his dedication to his school, his community, and his profession when you have occasion to meet with him or contact him.
- Let him know what you admire and respect about him, especially as they may relate to his beliefs and convictions.

- Appoint him as chair of a committee to study the incidence of sexually transmitted diseases and pregnancies of students in the district. Let him know that the committee's work and recommendations will be tantamount to reconsideration of his proposal.

(Adapted with permission from Kahler [1982, 1995].)

## REFERENCES

Blake, R. R., and J. S. Mouton. 1985. *The managerial grid III: A new look at the classic that has boosted productivity and profits for thousands of corporations worldwide.* Houston: Gulf Publishing.

Kahler, T. 1982. *Personality pattern inventory studies.* Little Rock, Ark.: Kahler Communications.

———. 1995. *The process teaching seminar.* Little Rock, Ark.: Kahler Communications.

———. 1996a. *The advanced process communication seminar.* Little Rock, Ark.: Kahler Communications.

———. 1996b. *The key to me seminar.* Little Rock, Ark.: Kahler Communications.

# SEVEN

# Pure Dreamer: Dorothy

Dorothy is an *imaginative, reflective,* and *calm* person. She decided to become an educator because she wanted a regular job with an established routine. Her life focuses inwardly. She prefers to reflect on things and issues and to envision what possibilities lay before her. Her home is functional and uncluttered. She has what she needs but is not prone to frills or anything overly done.

Dorothy experiences the world through her imagination and reflections. She prefers to be alone and work undisturbed. She is very good at doing repetitive tasks. Routines allow her to do her job with few interruptions or redirection. When she is asked a question or for information, she tends to respond directly and to the point. She is unlikely to embellish or elaborate on a response unless directed to do so. When working with others, she will provide the structure or template for the activity and give them "room" to work. She may encourage a discussion of issues but is unlikely to engage in the discussion herself to any great extent. Her reticence to interact to any great extent might give others the impression that she is overly shy or possibly unintelligent, but that is probably not the case. Her preference to be alone is not related to her abilities. In fact, she may be highly intelligent, needing direction from others to move into areas to use/expand her ideas but also needing private time and space to do so.

As an educational professional, Dorothy might gravitate to media or technology, areas where she would be able to direct learning without continual and active involvement. She would provide basic information for students to get started on a task. She might also use seatwork to reinforce the concepts she presents. She would expect students to be able to work independently with minimal direction or instructions. She is likely to work better with older students, who do not need a lot of contact.

Her approach to discipline would be to expect quiet work, without disturbing others. Those who are more outgoing will challenge Dorothy's patience and energy. She would likely exclude those who cannot or will not interact quietly (and minimally).

She needs *solitude*. That is, she needs time and space to be alone. She can move into other frames of preference, but the amount of energy she has to interact with others will depend on the amount of "alone" time she has had. She would prefer to be directed to take on an assignment or do a task; she will do likewise for those she supervises.

She finds her direction to act from others. She is very good with her hands and is likely to gravitate toward tactile tasks. She approaches her job with a sense of wanting to do well what she is directed to do. She would probably not initiate new projects but would participate as part of a team in the "wings." She would be an excellent recorder of ideas and might even share some of her thinking (when directed to do so). Her ability to reflect on things might give the group a stable and considered perspective.

She dresses without much consideration of style and in an unfussy way. She wears her hair simply and may not use much, if any, makeup. At a time when the gray begins to show, she would not obscure it. Some might describe her as "plain," but she would probably not take offense at the description and might even agree with it. On "dressy" occasions, she would dress appropriately but not overdo her appearance; however, she would prefer to avoid crowds and loud celebrations.

Dorothy will not actively seek recognition for her work or accolades for a job done well. As an administrator or supervisor, she is unlikely to do much in the way of acknowledging or rewarding good performance, but she is likely to be aware of problems that may occur. She will intercede only when absolutely necessary.

Dorothy is not likely to seek an administrative position on her own, but she might be drafted or recruited. A status quo organization that does not need much direction or leadership would work best for her. One that required a great deal of interaction would be distressful for her, and she would probably leave after a short period of time. She would more likely be a follower and a good team member. Her Blake-Mouton (1985) style is likely to be more in the direction of production than people.

Dorothy's preferred administrative style is *autocratic*—assigning tasks and duties. She will direct others to action but will not "micromanage" or supervise too closely. She will look to others to generate new ideas and will provide her feedback if she is responsible for the overall running of a program or project. Maintaining the status quo with established routines and procedures is her preference. It involves a minimum of interaction and planning.

Dorothy prefers a *directive* channel of communication. She will seek information straightforwardly in interchanges with others. She will also respond directly when asked for information—without embellishment, rationalization, or emotion.

If Dorothy has a life issue to resolve, it is likely to be *self-confidence* or *self-direction*. She may experience long-term intense distress with a focus on what might happen if she is not strong—"Things and people can make me feel bad. Therefore, I will be strong and withdraw, and as I become passive, I can avoid making my own decisions" (Kahler 1996a).

If she does not get her *solitude* needs met positively, she will retreat to a *be strong* driver position—protecting herself by "cocooning," or spreading herself too thinly. She will use the passive voice more than usual—"It occurred to me . . ." If Dorothy's distress continues, she will don a *Drooper* mask and withdraw. The warning signals are either her waiting passively or starting a number of things without finishing them.

This distress may carry over to her personal life. She may become more and more distant (even from those significant other people in her life), or appear embarrassed or shier than usual. She will wait passively to be directed by others—people or situations. When she is in distress, Dorothy's life is one of increased inaction. Her preeminent need for solitude overrides any interaction. The more others try to involve her in group activities or projects, the more she is likely to withdraw.

If Dorothy works with a supervisor whose preferences are different from hers or who are intolerant to hers, she is likely to appear disinterested in her job or uncommitted to the mission of the organization. The Thinkers and Believers with whom she works may distance themselves from her because of her inaction, or they may become fussy about her lack of initiative and commitment. The Feelers will *sense* her distress and try to help or "fix" her. Neither the criticism nor overattention will be as useful as her finding the solitude she needs.

## DOROTHY'S PROFILE

| | |
|---|---|
| Character Strengths: | Imaginative, reflective, calm |
| Perceptual Preference: | Inactions (reflections) |
| Communication Channel: | Directive |
| Psychological Need: | Solitude |
| Administrative Style: | Autocratic |
| Driver: | Be strong |
| Failure Mechanism: | Withdraws |
| Distress Mask: | Drooper |
| Life Issue: | Self-confidence |

(Adapted with permission from Kahler [1995, 1996b].)

## PROBLEM SITUATION

Dorothy, your media specialist, seems to be more withdrawn than usual. She has started several projects—putting her card catalog on-line, reinventorying the audiovisual equipment, and reviewing catalogs for new instructional videos—but has finished none of these projects, all of which have been suggested/requested by either you or the central office. Your annual book fair is under way, with parent volunteers needing direction from her and a constant flow of traffic through her normally quiet environment. More teachers are assigning research projects, bringing students to the library more frequently.

### Symptoms for Consideration

Dorothy is demonstrating that she is not getting the Dreamer *solitude* she needs. Too-frequent interaction with others has put the media specialist into distress—parents wanting to know where to go, students asking questions about where to find materials, potential book buyers wandering through the library, and so on.

### Suggestions for Action

- Give her a day off—report it as either sick ("mental health") or personal (with her permission) leave. Doing this on a Monday or Friday would be best, since she would be away for at least three days.
- Assign her a reliable parent volunteer to oversee the book fair, so she would not have to have direct interaction with those who are participating—either as sellers or buyers.
- Tell her you are thinking about an academic service component for the curriculum involving student research and want to assign students (yours or others from a higher level in the district) as research methodology resource people. Tell her to prepare a plan to expand this idea so you can see how she envisions such a project. You want to review the plan with the pros and cons, and her oversight before you and she discuss whether it is feasible to implement.
- If she does not already have a private office with a door she can close, provide her with one. If she does, arrange to have one-way glass installed so she can see out but others cannot see into her office.

(Adapted with permission from Kahler [1982, 1995].)

### REFERENCES

Blake, R. R., and J. S. Mouton. 1985. *The managerial grid III: A new look at the classic that has boosted productivity and profits for thousands of corporations worldwide.* Houston: Gulf Publishing.

Kahler, T. 1982. *Personality pattern inventory studies.* Little Rock, Ark.: Kahler Communications.

————. 1995. *The process teaching seminar.* Little Rock, Ark.: Kahler Communications.

————. 1996a. *The advanced process communication seminar.* Little Rock, Ark.: Kahler Communications.

————. 1996b. *The key to me seminar.* Little Rock, Ark.: Kahler Communications.

# EIGHT

## Pure Funster: Angie

Angie is a *spontaneous*, *playful*, and *creative* person. (Her given name is Angela Marie, but only her mother calls her that.) She decided to become an educator because she liked the idea and thought it would be fun. Her life focuses outwardly. She prefers to react to things and issues, knowing quickly what she likes and what she does not. Her home is exciting but may appear chaotic to those who see the world through more orderly lenses. The rooms are bright and stimulating.

Angie experiences the world through her likes and dislikes (reactions). She prefers to be around others who will stimulate her and to work in an exciting environment—both physically and intellectually. She is very good at coming up with very creative—some might say, "bizarre"—approaches to situations. Routines bore her. She prefers to work on projects that are exciting—if they are also fun, even better. When she is asked a question or for information, she tends to react spontaneously—sometimes without thinking through the issue.

She prefers to be around others with high energy. When working with students, she will assign them work mostly according to the curriculum or scope-and-sequence chart, but will embellish the presentation in a fun way if she can. She may facilitate a discussion of issues but is likely to encourage creative thinking—sometimes, the more outlandish, the better. Her preference to interact in fun ways may give others (usually Thinkers and Believers) the impression she is not focused or dedicated to the educational venture because her approach is definitely in the minority. Her preference for contact and in a stimulating environment is related to her ability to "color outside the lines." In fact, she may be

87

highly intelligent, sometimes needing permission to tap into her store of creativity.

As a teacher, Angie might gravitate to art, music, or drama—areas where she would be able to emote and to stimulate others to do likewise. She would provide basic information for students to get started on a task, but she is likely to expect them to think divergently some of the time. She would expect students to be able to interact with others and devise group projects as part of the learning environment. She is likely to work better with students who prefer a lot of contact and who are willing to look at things differently. Students who require structure and direction will have difficulty with Angie's style. In fact, they may find her energy tiresome . . . and tiring. Similarly, Angie may become frustrated—even sarcastic—with students who are reluctant to explore their creative side.

Her approach to discipline would be to joke and, possibly, tease good-naturedly first. Those who are more outgoing will appeal to Angie, but they may also distract and redirect the lesson. Her classroom is likely to be noisy and busy. The rules for behavior are probably few and typically unenforced. Serious disrupters of activities would be difficult for Angie to redirect. She would be more likely to argue with them. She would need assistance with those who misbehaved chronically. She would also place the "blame" on them for acting badly, even though they might be responding to her style or environment.

She needs *contact*. That is, she needs to be around people and situations that are exciting and stimulating. She can move into other frames of preference, but the amount of energy she has to interact with others will depend on the amount of "fun" time she has had. She would prefer to be delegated an assignment or do a task; she will do likewise for those she supervises. This delegation would be interpreted as "do it the way *you* want. It's your project." However, if a project delegated to her is accompanied by structure or specific parameters, they may get in the way of Angie's approach or creativity.

She finds her motivation to act from other people and things. She is very good with her hands and is probably very coordinated, especially with fine-motor tasks. She approaches her job with a sense of excitement and challenge. She will probably initiate new projects that allow her to flex her creativity. She would participate as part of a team of her "buddies." She would be an excellent generator of ideas—especially highly creative ones. Her ability to react to things might be difficult for the rest of the group, especially those who need and want structure and logical thinking—but they would not usually be within her circle of colleagues. Angie would be very good in brainstorming situations. She would be someone who searches for alternatives, going beyond the known and the obvious and the satisfactory. She would prefer movement into new territory instead of judgment, tradition, and clarity. Angie has a strong ability to think *laterally*—cutting across established patterns to generate new concepts and perceptions.

She dresses without consideration of style or the organization. She is likely to attract attention with her nonconformity. She might appear rumpled or unkempt—or unironed. Her clothes are likely to be bright—and maybe uncoordinated. The colors she chooses may be loud—especially her hair and nail polish. Responses from those who think/believe there is/ought to be a dress code might be, "How can she dress like that? Doesn't she know how important appearance and image are in education?" If she does dress up or dress down, she would be playing a role. If it is fun for her, she will do it.

Angie will not actively seek recognition for her work or accolades for a job done well. As an administrator or supervisor, she is likely to give "high fives" as a way of acknowledging or rewarding good performance, but she would have to move to another part of her personality to offer more traditional recognition—letters, certificates, plaques, and so on.

Angie's preferred administrative style is laissez-faire. She will delegate tasks to others but will not micromanage or supervise too closely. She will look to others to generate new ideas and will interact with them if they ask for her involvement and feedback. Maintaining the status quo with established routines and procedures is boring to her. She would prefer to test new areas of solution. She will be stymied often in traditional organizations and will leave a dull situation in favor of someplace more exciting. (Since Angie operates freely, she is like to be focused externally—outside of traditional "lines." Her Blake-Mouton [1985] orientation would be toward the 1,1 position of being disengaged. This does not reflect a lack of commitment to the organization, only that she will supervise from a distance.)

Angie prefers an *emotive* channel of communication. She interacts energetically in interchanges with others. When asked for information, she will respond playfully, but will eventually get to the point—especially if others seem exasperated with her less-than-direct attitude.

If Angie has a life issue to resolve, it is likely to be *self-love*. She may experience long-term intense distress with a focus on what might happen if she does not try hard to understand—"If you don't do the thinking for me, then I won't be happy. Therefore, I will try hard. When you don't make me feel good by thinking for me, then it's your fault I feel bad, and as long as I blame you, I can avoid the responsibility of feeling good with self-love" (Kahler 1996a).

If she does not get her *contact* needs met positively, she will retreat to a *try hard* driver position—feigning confusion and inviting others to think for her: "I don't get it." She will invite "games" more than usual—"Yes . . . but" is one of her favorites. (You offer her a solution that she seems to accept, but then invites you to offer another possibility or defend your idea: "Yes, I heard what you said, but . . .") If Angie's distress continues, she will don a *Blamer* mask and go to a position of "I'm OK; you're not." The warning signals are her becoming negative and complaining, blameless, or blameful.

This distress may carry over to her personal life. She may become more and more irresponsible, and blame others when things go awry. She will expect others to make things right—"After all, it was their *fault* in the first place." When she is in distress, Angie's life is one of blaming. Her preeminent need for contact takes on a negative air. The more others try to rationalize and be logical, the more she is likely to blame: "See what you made me do."

If Angie works with a supervisor whose preferences are different from hers or who is intolerant to hers, she is likely to sabotage her job or a project as a way of getting the contact she needs—even if it is negative. The Thinkers and Believers with whom she works may find her "irresponsible" behavior to be exasperating or frustrating, and they will become fussy about her lack of commitment and obeying the rules. The Feelers will *sense* her distress and try to help or "fix" her. Neither the criticism nor overattention will be as useful as her finding the contact she needs.

## ANGIE'S PROFILE

Character Strengths:      Spontaneous, creative, playful
Perceptual Preference:      Reactions (likes and dislikes)
Communication Channel:    Emotive
Psychological Need:        Contact (playful)
Administrative Style:       Laissez-faire
Driver:                  Try hard
Failure Mechanism:         Blames
Distress Mask:             Blamer
Life Issue:               Self-love

(Adapted with permission from Kahler [1995, 1996b].)

## PROBLEM SITUATION

Angie, your art teacher, is consistently late with attendance reports; she even turns them in occasionally using artist drawing pencil—smudged and illegible. She is not supervising the comings and goings of students from her room carefully. Recently, there was a scuffle between two students outside of her room. Two other teachers farther away had to separate the students. When you, as her supervisor, asked her why she did not attend to the situation, her response was, "Oh, I didn't realize they needed my help."

### Symptoms for Consideration

By acting irresponsibly, Angie is giving you definite clues that her Funster needs of playful *contact* are not being met. She may be too mired in the routine of school—filling out reports, providing a structured environment for students, and so forth. She is not having the energizing fun she needs to charge her batteries.

### Suggestions for Action

- Make contact with Angie at the next opportunity with some high energy—"Cool outfit!" "Wow! I didn't know you could walk by putting one foot in front of the other." (Be careful that the message or the tone is not teasing or sarcastic but more of a playful observation. You may see the jargon and playfulness as "silly," but Angie will like this type of *contact*.)

- Ask her to redecorate some aspect of the building in need of a new look, and give her free rein to do it. (If you are afraid of something too bizarre, provide some gentle but not-too-restrictive parameters.)
- Ask her to serve as a resource person/advisor to any of the school activities or productions requiring a creative approach. Do not assign her these tasks, but give her the option of participating when she can contribute and *enjoy* herself.
- If you need help with a very kinesthetic program (dance, athletics/ recreation, carnival), be sure she is on the committee or ask her to participate in helping to be sure everyone has a good time.

(Adapted with permission from Kahler [1982, 1995].)

### REFERENCES

Blake, R. R., and J. S. Mouton. 1985. *The managerial grid III: A new look at the classic that has boosted productivity and profits for thousands of corporations worldwide*. Houston: Gulf Publishing.

Kahler, T. 1982. *Personality pattern inventory studies*. Little Rock, Ark.: Kahler Communications.

———. 1995. *The process teaching seminar*. Little Rock, Ark.: Kahler Communications.

———. 1996a. *The advanced process communication seminar*. Little Rock, Ark.: Kahler Communications.

———. 1996b. *The key to me seminar*. Little Rock, Ark.: Kahler Communications.

# NINE

## Pure Doer: Doug

It is noteworthy that in hundreds of profiles completed for educators, less than 1 percent has a Doer base. Some educators may be in Doer phase, but again in much lower proportions than in the general population. It is not uncommon to see upper-level decision makers that are Believer base in Doer phase. (Refer back to chapter 3, "Communication Blueprints," for the base and phase concepts.) This chapter speaks to what one is likely to find in the Doer personality.

Doug is an *adaptable, persuasive,* and *charming* person. (His given name is "Robert Douglas," but he prefers to be called "Doug.") He decided to become an educator because he anticipated he would find an active and stimulating work environment. His life focuses outwardly. He prefers action and quick payoffs—getting to the "bottom line" and completing projects. His home reflects the outward trappings of an active lifestyle. The rooms are colorful and filled with "trophies"—stuffed animals from hunting, expensive furniture, exercise equipment, and possibly trendy artwork.

Doug experiences the world through actions. He prefers to get into projects that will be completed in short order, and to work in an environment where rewards are quick in coming. He is very good at cutting through red tape and finding fast routes to intermediate goals. Routines bore him. He prefers to work on projects that lead to tangible rewards; if they are also interesting, that is OK but not necessary. When he is asked a question or for information, he tends to respond directly. He is not likely to explain or rationalize things unless someone else pursues an issue or topic. He will talk in jargon and action words and will use nicknames or pseudo endearments when addressing others: "Hey, babe [which might be interpreted as sexist, but he might use it with men, too]. Let's get this show going. We've got to get things done."

He prefers to be around others who prefer short-term attainment. When working with students, he will assign them work that can be completed quickly, but will not spend a lot of time providing extensive feedback or much rationale of the importance of the work. Format and details are not as important as the overall assignment. He may plan a discussion of issues but is likely to encourage moving to resolution or solution quickly. His preference for the bottom line may give others the impression he is not committed or dedicated to the educational venture—that impression may be accurate to some degree. His preference for action and short-term outcomes is related to his ability to get things done. He may be highly intelligent, but his lack of attention to detail many times may lead others to assume he is not dependable and focused only on what he can get out of a project.

As a teacher, Doug might gravitate to vocational subjects or physical education, areas where he and his students would be active. He would provide basic information for students to get started on a task, but he is likely to want them to move quickly to demonstrating skill development or project completion. He would allow students to interact with others, especially if they could accomplish things more quickly that way. He is likely to work better with students who are oriented kinesthetically— that is, students similar to him. Students who require structure and direction will have difficulty with Doug's style. In fact, they may find his bottom-line preference ill placed and confusing. Similarly, Doug may become frustrated—even cynical—with students who persevere with their work, that is, those who take whatever time they need or who are not satisfied quickly.

His approach to breaches of discipline (misbehavior) would be to manipulate compliance/redirection first. Those who are canny and smooth in extricating themselves from trouble will appeal to Doug. His classroom is likely to be busy and outcome oriented. The rules for behavior are probably few and typically unenforced. Serious disrupters of activities would meet with vindictiveness. He would be likely to set them up to fail or be excluded from the classroom. He would not have time for those who misbehave. He would also place the "blame" on them for acting badly, even though they might be responding to his style or environment—or to a situation he had orchestrated.

Doug needs *incidence*. That is, he needs lots of opportunities for action and payoffs. He can move into other frames of preference, but the amount of energy he has to interact with others will depend on the number of things he has accomplished and the "wealth" (tangible or psychological) he has accumulated from them. He would prefer to be directed to an assignment or do a task; he will do likewise for those he supervises. However, he is likely to move ahead with decisions without consulting others. A typical approach he would see as positive because it would get things done is, "Do what is necessary and rationalize/apologize for it later." As a senior administrator, he is not likely to be questioned for his decision making, unless the outcomes are less than salutary for the organization. His subordinates would find most of his decisions falling into Barnard's (1938) "zone of indifference"—that is, there might not be a strong commitment to the decision, but it would be carried out nevertheless. His parental style will disenfranchise others in the organization, and his "my-way-or-the-highway" attitude will leave him with few close colleagues.

He finds his motivation to act from others. He is very kinesthetic and extrinsically motivated. He approaches his job with a sense of challenge and seeks tangible accomplishments. He will probably focus on perfecting behaviors that will bring him the payoffs he seeks. He would participate as part of a team of his "buddies," especially if they were mutually outcome oriented. He is not likely to generate new ideas, unless they will help him accomplish things more quickly. His preference for the bottom line might be difficult for the rest of the group, especially those who need and want structure and logical thinking—but they would not usually be within his circle of associates. Doug would be very good in finding the quickest way to get a project finished, but he might "overlook" some of the details in getting there. He would need the assistance of Angie to generate creative solutions, Dorothy to carry out the mundane operations, and Alfred or Matthew to attend to the details. Without their assistance, he would flounder as an administrator and, possibly, "fail" or be encouraged to move on to another job or organization.

He dresses flamboyantly. He is likely to attract attention with his flaunting style. He might have bold jewelry. His clothes are likely to be trendy—even provocative. The colors he chooses would be reds and blacks. Others (again, usually the Thinkers and Believers) in the organization would see his style as inappropriate. They might suggest he tone down his appearance, if they were directed by him to "Tell me how I look." He would not change and would discount/disregard negative responses.

Doug will actively seek rewards for his work or tangible acknowledgment for a job done well. As an administrator or supervisor, he is likely to provide incentives as a way of stimulating productivity. He would give monetary rewards if he had discretionary monies available, or might look for benefactors outside of the organization.

Doug's preferred administrative style is *autocratic*. He will delegate the detail work to others but will not micromanage or supervise too closely. Maintaining the status quo with routines and procedures is boring to him, unless there is a consistent pattern of rewards and payoffs connected with established practice. He would prefer to pursue a new route or create new alliances to move toward organizational productivity. (He, like Dorothy, would prefer more of a task orientation.) He will be stymied often in traditional organizations and may flit from one to another in search of tangible rewards. Since he prefers action, he would be seen as a *change agent*. Because change is highly uncomfortable, especially in educational organizations, Doug would be frustrated quickly if he could not effect change—and he would move on.

Doug prefers a *directive* channel of communication. When he is energized and OK, he interacts straightforwardly in interchanges with others. When asked for information, he will respond directly, without embellishment or the need to explain. However, he might try to manipulate a situation that was not going his way, even being seductive in the attempt.

If Doug has a life issue to resolve, it is likely to be *bonding*. He may experience long-term intense distress with a focus on what might happen if others are not strong—"Things and people can make you feel bad. Therefore, you will have to be strong and abandon anyone who gets too close. As long as I abandon you, I can avoid bonding with you" (Kahler 1996).

If he does not get his *incidence* needs met positively, he will retreat to a *"you have to be strong"* driver position—being unsupportive and expecting others to fend for themselves. If Doug's distress continues, he will don a *Blamer* mask and go to a position of "I'm OK; you're not." He will set up negative drama—attempting to get others into arguments or disagreements as a way of achieving the incidence he needs. The warning signals are his ignoring or breaking rules or trying to get them changed for himself only. He will say "You . . ." when talking about himself—"You know when you're driving down the highway and going fast, you have to look out for the 'fuzz.'" (Meaning: "When I am driving down the highway too fast, I have to watch for radar or police." But then he probably has a radar detector as one of his "car toys.")

This distress may carry over to his personal life. He may become more and more manipulative and take high risks. He may use alcohol and drugs to excess. He might be seductive to achieve an end. He will expect others to "take it." When they do not, his response would be "Ah hah! I knew they weren't strong enough." When he is in distress, Doug's life is one of blaming. His preeminent need for incidence takes on a negative air. The more others try to redirect him, the more manipulative and defensive he is likely to be.

If Doug works with a supervisor whose preferences are different from his or who are intolerant to his, he is likely to create some negative drama—getting others to argue and become competitive with each other. The Thinkers and Believers with whom he works would find his manipulative behavior unacceptable, and they will avoid him and distance themselves from him if possible. The Feelers will try to help him, but they are likely to be seduced and hurt. Neither the criticism nor overadaptation will work. Doug will become productive only if he finds incidence in his professional and personal life.

## DOUG'S PROFILE

| | |
|---|---|
| Character Strengths: | Adaptable, persuasive, charming |
| Perceptual Preference: | Actions |
| Communication Channel: | Directive |
| Psychological Need: | Incidence |
| Administrative Style: | Autocratic |
| Driver: | You must be strong |

| Failure Mechanism: | Manipulates |
| Distress Mask: | Blamer |
| Life Issue: | Bonding |

(Adapted with permission from Kahler [1995, 1996].)


## PROBLEM SITUATION

Doug is new to your staff, with five years of previous experience. His classroom is very active from what you have seen so far. It is a very rainy day, and you, the principal, notice that your new teacher, Doug, is parking in the space designated clearly, "Teacher of the Year." This is a prominent space, close to the school entrance and reserved for another faculty member, who was selected for the distinction by the rest of the faculty.


### Symptoms for Consideration

Doug obviously is not respecting the reserved parking space or the reason it was reserved in the first place. He has "broken the rules," manipulated the situation to suit himself. His actions may precipitate a confrontation—between him and the "Teacher of the Year," with you as possible referee (negative drama). He is demonstrating Doer distress of not getting his *incidence* needs met through his manipulation and expects others to *be strong* as a way of coping and accommodating. He is likely to attempt to be charming and possibly seductive when he is approached, and will probably downplay the importance of this breach of etiquette or protocol with, "It was raining real hard and I thought you wouldn't mind if I *borrowed* your space." He might also attempt to pacify his colleague with promise of a future "reward," which is unlikely ever to be proffered.


### Suggestions for Action

- Do a "one-minute reprimand," à la *The One Minute Manager* (Blanchard and Johnson 1982): "That space is reserved for the

'Teacher of the Year.' Don't park there again until you have attained the honor." Do not preach or explain the importance of the award. (Document the action in a "memorandum of understanding" to emphasize your point, thanking Doug for his cooperation. Note also that you will have to be direct with Doug. He will not perceive your directness as being rude; however, being direct—using an *autocratic* style—may not be the way you usually handle situations. In this case, you will connect with the teacher and invite him to change more effectively than any of the other interaction styles.)

- Invite Doug to submit a plan for competition for other parking spaces to be reserved or other "perks" for performance.

(Adapted with permission from Kahler [1982, 1995].)

## REFERENCES

Barnard, C. I. 1938. *The functions of the executive*. Cambridge, Mass.: Harvard University Press.

Blanchard, K. H., and S. Johnson. 1982. *The one-minute manager*. New York: Berkley Books.

Gilbert, M. B. 1994. Meeting communication needs of students can promote success. Little Rock: University of Arkansas at Little Rock. (Unpublished report of Off-Campus Duty Assignment)

———. 1999. Why educators have problems with some students: Understanding frames of preference. *Journal of Educational Administration* 37: 243–55. ERIC, EJ 592943.

Kahler, T. 1982. *Personality pattern inventory studies*. Little Rock, Ark.: Kahler Communications.

———. 1994. *The advanced process communication seminar*. Little Rock, Ark.: Kahler Communications.

———. 1995. *The process teaching seminar*. Little Rock, Ark.: Kahler Communications.

———. 1996. *The key to me seminar*. Little Rock, Ark.: Kahler Communications.

# Section III

## PUTTING THINGS TOGETHER: BUILDING EFFECTIVE COMMUNICATION SKILLS

# TEN

## Dealing with Conflict

Many successful builders have their special tools and techniques. It may be a favorite hammer, a specific location on a job site to start laying brick, or a way to finish a joint.

Effective leaders have their favorite "tools," too. In most cases, these leaders prefer to stick to the tools or methods that have worked in the past—this is a useful way to address situations that are similar to others they have faced before.

The problem is that the favorite "hammer" may not work well all of the time. It may be too heavy for some finishing work or too cumbersome for a delicate job. A lighter "tool" might be better—and more effective.

### PREPARATION

Administrators prepare for their jobs in two ways—formally and informally. The formal preparation comes through course work at colleges and universities, and through other organized activities such as workshops and readings. Informal preparation comes through life experience. We take what we have learned and apply it in situations where it seems appropriate, or we observe others doing things effectively and try to emulate their methods. But not all situations can be resolved using the same approach, even if it has worked before. When we use an approach that does not work, then we might try it again, find a different approach, ask or tell someone else to do it, ignore the situation, or give up.

Of course, repeating an approach that has not worked usually meets with similar results. Finding a different way to resolve a conflict is useful but may be time consuming. Giving in to someone else or ignoring the circumstances removes the situation from our immediate concern. Giving up does little more than put the situation aside without resolution.

In more formal terms, there are a number of techniques to manage conflict: *avoidance, suppression, domination, compromise,* and *integration* (or problem solving). The behaviors and their rubrics are listed in table 10.1. (With the Blake-Mouton [1985] Model, the first number represents relative *concern for production*, and the second number signifies relative *concern for people*—or focus on tasks or focus on relationships. By example, one who tends to *suppress* conflict has a low degree of concern for production and a high degree of concern for people.)

By using the first four techniques, the administrator does little more than manage the situation. If there is conflict, it is set aside—for a time. Using *integration*—the conflict management style that seeks creative alternatives—is the only true way to *resolve* conflict. The leader who adopts this style has a high degree of concern for both people and production and uses a team approach to problem solving.

## MANAGING CONFLICT

### What Is Conflict?

Conflict occurs when people interacting with each other *perceive* their goals to be incompatible. Here, perception is reality. Whether or

**Table 10.1   Conflict Management Styles**

| Conflict Mgt. Style | Behaviors | Blake-Mouton Style |
|---|---|---|
| Avoidance | Giving up/withdrawing | 1,1 |
| Suppression | Ignoring/denying/smoothing | 1,9 |
| Domination | Telling someone else | 9,1 |
| Compromise | Finding alternatives | 5,5 |
| Integration | Finding creative alternatives | 9,9 |

not the goals are truly incompatible is overshadowed by how people see the situation—each through his or her own screens. (This is akin to the communication screens shown in the communication rainbow in chapter 2.) When we bring different perceptions to a conflict, we may have difficulty empathizing or seeing things through someone else's lenses.

Conflict arises for various reasons:

- Ambiguous roles
- Conflicting interests
- Communication barriers
- Dependence of one party (on another)
- Differentiation of organization (causing confusion or imbalance of authority)
- Need for consensus
- Behavior regulations or rules
- Unresolved prior conflicts (Maurer 1991, 3–4)

Moreover, if we perceive we have incompatible goals, we may want to *win*: win our position, win the day, or simply get what we want, regardless of the needs of others. Conflict does not go away without the parties agreeing that it is gone. It is gone only when the situation turns into *win win*.

### What May Not Be Effective

If one of the resolutions to conflict is losing, then the conflict is not resolved. Different types of people need to be approached differently when they are in conflict. Their personality types will describe patterns that may help them get what they need, possibly overriding the situation. That is, their needs will overshadow the situation—shifting the focus to themselves and away from the problem. The likelihood is that they are in distress and will show the predictable patterns described for the six people you have just met.

Another way to look at unresolved conflict is to consider that the participants are not getting their needs met. This is the *distress* (or miscommunication) component of the Process Communication Model (Kahler 1982). The first degree is the *driver* behavior we may see many times during a day. It is mild and indicates the beginning of distress. If the lack of need fulfillment continues and gets more pronounced, we may see a second degree of distress. This is where each personality will don a mask. Someone in the interaction will be seen as "not OK," and a particular conflict management style will emerge.

*Avoidance* takes Feelers and Dreamers out of the situation or puts the situation aside. The conflict is not resolved; they just are not a part of it anymore: "I am not going to deal with this," Dreamer Dorothy might say as she withdraws in an attempt to get her need for *solitude* met.

Barbara (the Feeler) will be distressed at the conflict, especially if she is involved directly. She either will attempt to appease ("I just want everyone to be happy.") or overadapt ("How can I make this better for you?"), trying to find acceptance of herself as a person.

> Barbara (Feeler): "Dorothy, would it be possible to postpone putting the library collection on computer . . . for a while? It's probably my fault that we are moving ahead, but I am uncomfortable with the confusion it may bring to the staff."
>
> Dorothy (Dreamer): (Silence)
>
> Barbara: "I know we talked about this and I really appreciate all you have

**Table 10.2   Distress Patterns, Conflict Style, and Masks**

| Personality | First Degree | Second Degree | Conflict Mgt. | Mask |
|---|---|---|---|---|
| Feeler | Overadapts | Invites criticism | Avoidance; Suppression | Drooper (I'm not OK) |
| Thinker | Does not delegate | Overcontrols | Domination; Compromise | Attacker (You're not OK) |
| Believer | Focuses negatively | Pushes beliefs | Domination; Compromise | Attacker (You're not OK) |
| Dreamer | Does not finalize | Withdraws | Avoidance | Drooper (I'm not OK) |
| Funster | Delgates inappropriately | Blames | Suppression; Domination | Blamer (You're not OK) |
| Doer | Does not support | Manipulates | Suppression; Domination | Blamer (You're not OK) |

[Adapted with permission from Kahler, T. (1982), and Kahler, T. (1996).]

done. . . . Oh my! Things are in such a mess. Would it be OK if we talked more later?"

Dorothy: "OK!"

*Suppression* denies the conflict exists: "You really don't hate your sister," Barbara would offer, trying to bring harmony into family chaos. (She sees the staff in her organization as extended family.) Angie, the Funster, might look for ways to get her playful contact need met by ignoring the conflict: "Oh, yeah! Well, we can't deal with that now. We have other fish to fry."

> Barbara (Feeler): "I hate to interrupt. I know you are planning for your new project. I am a bit uneasy about the blank space, so I am wondering, how will you design the walls? I know it's a bother, but I need to order the paint."
>
> Angie (Funster): "Yeah, I know I did promise, but I have a super idea. How about giving students the paint and letting them come up with their own design?"
>
> Barbara: "Oh, I don't know. I am not sure if that would work—giving them free rein like that. I mean, you are so creative and everything . . ."
>
> Angie: "Aw, c'mon. It'll be fun—and the students can be as creative as they want."

An individual who relies on *domination* to manage conflict attempts to control behavior by dictating the approach to resolve (not really) the conflict in which one party wholly *wins* and the other party *loses*. "Here's what *we*'re going to do . . ." action-oriented Doug would assert, trying to cut through any protracted discussion and get to the bottom line. Someone in a position of power (or perceived power) and who is willing to use that power to get what he or she wants uses this technique. The other party is given little choice but to follow the dictum. (This will work in many situations unless the order falls into the *zone of noncompliance* [Barnard 1938]. Noncompliance may be tantamount to subversion or insubordination. At times, orders clash sharply with the personal values of people, and they cannot obey.)

> Doug (Doer): "Ya know. Let's just scrap the policy manual and start over."

Matthew (Believer): "What?! Do you mean to tell me you want to throw
away all of what we've been doing all these years?"

Doug: "Yeah! That stuff's not working anyway. Ya know when you're looking for an answer, you rarely find it in that policy manual. You gotta go
where the action is."

Matthew: "I am not sure this is the way to proceed. Specifically, what are
you proposing?"

Doug: "We're gonna start from scratch, and too bad for anyone who
doesn't like it."

*Compromise* is characterized by each party giving up something in
order to reach a decision or to move on: "I'll meet you halfway." Alfred,
our Thinker, and Matthew, our Believer, will approach the issue of incompatible goals rationally and try to reason through the situation. This
will address the recognition of their work they both need: "If the conflict is resolved, you will see me in a good light." Alfred's *good* work is
recognized; Matthew's contribution to organizational goals will be seen
as important. As a result of the agreement, Alfred will be able to move
on to the other things in his full schedule (time structure), and Matthew
will have some of his conviction need met.

While this does allow the deal to be closed or the issue to be put aside,
the goals that led to the conflict still may be incompatible. Since neither
party was fully satisfied, the conflict—the incompatible goals—may resurface if the individuals have an ongoing relationship.

Union negotiations provide a good example of this. It is highly unlikely that unions get all they want for their members in a bargaining
agreement. They typically ask for more than they know they will get,
and organizations usually offer less than they know they will have to
give. This pattern underpins the unwritten bargaining "rules." As a result, the incompatible goals likely will arise when the next contract rene-
gotiation surfaces. In this example of *interdependence*, the conflicting
parties depend on each other because they often work together.

I remember how perplexed a colleague of mine was when he followed
the "rules" in what appeared to be a negotiation. He asked for a certain
position, and the other party thought it was reasonable. His response
was, "I should have asked for more," even though he got what he
wanted.

Alfred (Thinker): "We need to resolve the situation about health clinics at the high school."

Matthew (Believer): "I don't believe this community is ready for our interference in family matters."

Alfred: "How about if I come up with a plan that I think the community will accept?"

Matthew: "If you mean working on this by yourself, what exactly is your plan? Will you pass it by me first? I would like a chance to review it."

These are all techniques used by administrators. More effective leaders look for more lasting resolution.

### Resolving Conflict Integratively

The first four techniques of managing conflict truly do not resolve the situation. Instead, they may allow us to put the situation aside for the time being. The true *win-win* outcome can only be reached integratively.

In resolution through *integration*, both parties contribute and neither party gives up anything to arrive at a result. One of the earliest proponents of this strategy was Mary Parker Follett. She saw true resolution of conflict to be achieved through cooperation, collaboration, and collegiality. "Integration involves invention, and the clever thing is to recognize this, and not to let one's thinking stay within the boundaries of two alternatives which are mutually exclusive" (Follett in Metcalf and Urwick 1940, 33).

Empowerment is the key to using integration effectively. It is the use of power *with* colleagues, coworkers, and subordinates rather than power *over* them.

Many experts in the field of organizational theory have explored the notion of power in organizations. Perhaps the most famous view of power comes from Max Weber (1947). He saw power as being both positional and attributional—related to who we are in the organization or who we are as people. When power is abused or misused in interactions, people may assume positions of dominance or submission.

From a transactional analysis (the basis of Process Communication) perspective, these positions are either "I'm OK; you're not OK" (dominance) or "I'm not OK; you're OK" (submission). If "I'm OK and you're not," I am assuming the role of a *persecutor* looking for a *victim* (Karpman 1968). These roles emerge during the distress described by Process Communication when the needs of Thinkers, Believers, Funsters, and Doers are not met positively (Kahler 1978).

If "I'm not OK and you are," I am a *victim* looking for a *persecutor* (Karpman 1968). This is the role of Feelers and Dreamers in distress (Kahler 1978). An imbalance of power can magnify distress.

Organizationally, power is the *ability to act*. This is combined with *authority* and *responsibility*—authority being the *right to act* and responsibility being the *obligation to act* (Corwin 1965). The effective leader shares authority through appropriate delegation, retaining ultimate responsibility. Power, then, describes both the physical and organizational ability of individuals to do their jobs.

It means sharing to the end of accomplishing a task. To achieve this shared empowerment, it is crucial for the parties to have mutual understanding of the task, the organization, and the goals. The appropriate use of *power, authority,* and *responsibility* may open the door to integration and keep people focused on resolving conflict positively. These are the tools of an effective leader.

## POINTS TO PONDER

- Conflict exists in all organization. Effective leaders must find ways to manage conflict or, even better, to resolve conflict.
- Conflict can serve to divide an organization, or it can be used to move organizations ahead.
- Recognizing that conflict is the perception of incompatible goals, leaders must seek the win-win position for lasting resolution.
- Integration of ideas and participation by the conflicted parties are the only ways to resolve conflict. All other methods of conflict management either ignore or set aside conflict for a period; the perceived incompatibility does not disappear.

## REFERENCES

Barnard, C. I. 1938. *The functions of the executive.* Cambridge, Mass.: Harvard University Press.

Blake, R. R., and J. S. Mouton. 1985. *The managerial grid III: A new look at the classic that has boosted productivity and profits for thousands of corporations worldwide*. Houston: Gulf Publishing.

Corwin, R. 1965. *A sociology of education: Emerging patterns of class, status, and power in the public schools*. New York: Appleton-Century-Crofts.

Kahler, T. 1978. *T. A. revisited*. Little Rock, Ark.: Human Development Publications.

———. 1982. *The process communication management seminar*. Little Rock, Ark.: Kahler Communications.

———. 1996. *Key to me for students profile*. Little Rock, Ark.: Kahler Communications.

Karpman, S. 1968. Fairy tales and script drama analysis. *Transactional Analysis Bulletin* 7 (26): 39–43.

Maurer, R. E. 1991. *Managing conflict: Tactics for school administrators*. Needham Heights, Mass.: Allyn and Bacon.

Metcalf, H. C., and L. Urwick, (eds.). 1940. *Dynamic administration: The collected papers of Mary Parker Follett*. New York: Harper and Row.

Weber, M. 1947. *The theory of social and economic organization*. Trans. by A. M. Henderson and T. Parsons. New York: Oxford University Press.

# ELEVEN

## Solving Problems Cooperatively: A Blueprint for Success

Conflict in organizations is inevitable. Resolving conflict and the problems that come from conflict is the true test of the effective leader. Succeeding as a conflict resolver brings into consideration three competencies of leadership:

- *Diagnosing,* the cognitive competency—understanding the situation.
- *Adapting,* the behavioral competency that helps close the gap between where things are and where you want them to be.
- *Communicating,* the process competency that allows others to understand and accept the situation and its need for resolution. (Hersey, Blanchard, and Johnson 1996)

At times, it may seem the situation cannot be resolved—deciding whether to go to your child's birthday party or attend an important professional conference, for example. If the dates for each are set and overlap, then you may have to choose.

What if another alternative will allow you to do both, but it would mean looking at the situation differently? It is this possibility that may allow you to be integrative—to get what you want without losing and not causing others to lose either. It may require you to think in a different way, putting aside the structure you have used before, which may have been to choose one event (usually the professional conference).

113

One way to do both of the above would be to go to the professional meeting and celebrate with your child when you return, even though it would be a different kind of celebration. You might also watch a videotape of the "party" and ask your child to describe the events.

We may settle for compromise because each party wins a bit, but each party also loses a bit. "Compromise does not create, it deals with what already exists; integration creates something new" (Follett in Metcalf and Urwick 1940, 35).

In integration, we find stability. The organization or relationship can progress because there is no residue from the conflict. However, we must be willing to be honest and open about the issue. We must trust and be willing to trust (an important concept in organizational effectiveness; see Ouchi 1982). "The first rule . . . for obtaining integration is to put your cards on the table, face the real issue, uncover the conflict, bring the whole thing into the open" (Follett in Urwick and Metcalf 1940, 38).

One problem here is that people may not be willing to be fully open or forthcoming if they fear that the other party to the conflict might use that information against them. That is, they are afraid to trust the other party because they might lose something—the argument, the issue at hand, the advantage. Withholding information can stymie the use of integration to resolve the conflict.

The differences that produce conflict can disrupt organizations. At the very least, they are distracting, but they can also be divisive. While something productive may arise from resolving conflict, there are some general guidelines to consider:

1. Differences are best resolved by those who differ, not by some third party.
2. The organization can function best when the authority system remains intact.
3. Wherever possible, let both sides win.
4. Memories are fallible; accept that fact.
5. Only the dead keep secrets. (Informal intraorganizational communication networks are usually very healthy.)
6. People hear what they want to hear and report the version they want known.

7. Some differences are irreconcilable. (Glatthorn and Adams 1983, 59–60)

Within organizations, there is an ongoing interdependence, the constant interaction that brings people together on a regular basis. There are few who operate independently. Hence, people work best when their differences are allayed, or when their differences do not interfere with operations, programs, or projects. When differences remain and are a continual source of conflict, more time may be spent on resolving problems than accomplishing the objectives of programs.

## DIAGNOSING

The way we normally think about, feel about, believe about, react to, reflect on, or act on a situation may limit our ability to perceive things differently. The boxes or compartments we know best provide us with preferred perceptions and interactions. When we accept that there are other ways to view things, then we begin the process of understanding multiple possibilities.

The conceptual blocks we may have are those barriers or impediments that hinder our perceiving a problem or conceiving its solution effectively. These blocks may be *perceptual* (limits on the way we process information), *emotional* (the fears and reactions that limit our affective responses), *cultural and environmental* (traditional and accepted patterns of response), and *intellectual and expressive* (lack of correct information or language) (Adams 1986).

To return to the condominium analogy (Kahler 1982) and the concept of shifting (moving into other frames of preference), we recall the sample personality structure we saw in chapter 3—the base Thinker in a Believer phase (perhaps this is Alfred). When we examine the graphic as shown again in figure 11.1, we also note some other things.

While Alfred is motivated currently by recognition of his work as being important and valuable and for his conviction, we also see that he has *staged* (completed a phase) through his Feeler. This means he has strength in accessing his emotions and can be sensitive to the feelings of others.

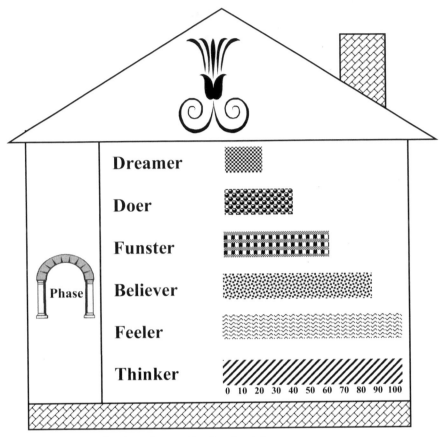

**Figure 11.1    Sample Phase Personality Condominium**

We also see something else. The floors above the Believer phase are less full, less "furnished." The amount of relative "energy" Alfred has is substantially less with each higher "floor."

When we access the preferences of another person and his or her personality type, we go to that floor in our structure. So when I want to be playful, I go to my Funster floor. I get there by way of an elevator.

Alfred has about 60 percent Funster "energy"—his Funster floor is about 60 percent furnished, a fair amount. If he has reason to tap into his Funster (go to his Funster floor), he will find sufficient tools to interact with someone needing *playful contact* and seeing the situation through *reactions.*

The reason he might *choose* to go there is because someone or something in his environment has invited him to do so. His son may want to play with him, or he may be asked to find a creative approach to a problem at work, or Angie may *need* for him to allow her to approach a situation creatively. Of course, as with any invitation, we can accept or reject it. If Alfred chooses to accept the invitation, he will have to "call" his elevator to get him there.

His ability to "call the elevator" depends on whether he is in distress or not. If Alfred (a base Thinker) is sufficiently motivated through recognition of his work and acceptance of his conviction (his Believer phase needs), he can push the call button, get on his elevator, and go to his Funster floor.

Recall the preferences discussed in chapter 3: When we have the need or desire to access different parts of who we are, we go to that floor of our personality.

- When I want to be logical, I go to my Thinker floor.
- When I want to be sensitive, I go to my Feeler floor.
- When I want to be dedicated, I go to my Believer floor.
- When I want to be reflective, I go to my Dreamer floor.
- When I want to be playful, I go to my Funster floor.
- When I want to be adaptable, I go to my Doer floor.

If Alfred's needs are not met, he will move through the predictable patterns of negative attempts to get the same needs met. He will not have the inclination to push the call button and will not go to his Funster floor. He will reject the invitation.

In this distress, we will see him interacting first with either the visual or virtual finger pointing of the "You have to be perfect to be OK" driver: "You got a 96 on that test. What exactly, precisely, happened to the other four points?" He will be hypercritical, focusing on what is wrong rather than what is right.

Continuing failure to get his needs met might bring out the Attacker mask. Alfred may become preachy, or crusade about what is important, with the overtone that anyone who disagrees is wrong: "You need to understand how important it is that you excel. Preparing well for the future is critical to your success in life." The end result is that he will not access his Funster. He will reject the invitation from his son to play, thereby setting up possible distress for his son, whose (playful) contact need will not be met with his father.

As we look further at the condominium, we note that Alfred's Doer and Dreamer floors are very sparsely furnished. Interacting with Doers or Dreamers from *their* perspective and through *their* preferences will be somewhat difficult for him. He may access his Doer or Dreamer, but he will not do so for long because of limited energy.

As Alfred runs out of energy, he will invite others to get in their elevators and move to a floor where he has more energy, such as his Believer. If the other person has sufficient Believer energy, a productive interaction is likely. However, if the other person has as little Believer energy as Alfred has Dreamer energy, then a meeting that focuses on values and opinions is not going to last long.

While our condominiums are "constructed" by the time we are seven years old, only the order of the floors is set. The amount of furnishing—the degree of energy—may change during our lives. This will occur with repeated visits to those sparsely furnished floors. When we go there time and time again, we bring more "furniture" and leave it there for our next visit.

Interestingly, once we have furnished a floor, it tends to stay furnished. Increased energy comes from experience and accepted invitations. The more we interact with others whose preferences are represented on our upper floors, the better those floors are furnished.

As we confront problems in our lives, we need to find an approach that works—one that will resolve the conflict and solve the problem. Here is a potential model for addressing problems:

- Define the problem.
- Acknowledge what, if any, additional information you need.
- Determine the urgency so that the situation can be considered with other priorities.
- Examine alternatives, looking at the pros and cons of each. (It is very important to consider both the positive and negative aspects, so you can see the benefits and the liabilities as you make a decision.)
- Decide which approach you will take.

- Propose a plan to implement.
- Implement the plan.
- Consider how you will determine if your approach has been effective: Was the problem solved? Is the conflict resolved? (This important step is often ignored.)

This straightforward approach has been proposed similarly by many others (Bolton 1979; Gamble and Gamble 1982; Glatthorn and Adams 1983; Maurer 1991, Hersey, Blanchard, and Johnson 1996). This model is very useful if you are a singular decision maker. If it is more than your problem, then the approach takes on other layers. That is, when you might involve others, you will need to consider their perspectives and preferences, their professional/organizational and personal maturity, and the urgency of the situation.

### Define the Problem

As I alluded in the preface, one of the first things we must do is decide who owns the problem. At times a frustrated teacher may barge into the principal's office: "Here! You deal with him! I am out of patience and have other students who need my attention." You have had someone else's problem dropped on your doorstep. You can choose to deal with it—or not.

If you choose to deal with it, then you have assumed some ownership. You have agreed tacitly that you will be involved directly. Someone else's "monkey" (the problem) is now in your care.

On the other hand, you might agree to provide a "cooling-off" place for the alleged miscreant, without delving further into the situation. You understand that the teacher has not been able to keep the student on task or to redirect inappropriate behavior, but you acknowledge the problem is truly the teacher's or the student's. If you refuse to intervene, then you have set the pattern that the problem is to be addressed at the source, if possible.

Once the determination has been made regarding ownership of the problem, then the focus can shift to problem definition. From the outset, defining the problem should be done with an eye to solution. The more contentious the situation, the more likely some people may want to *blame* or place unfulfilled responsibility. Of course, this is more cathartic than productive and may lead to arguments that inhibit or prohibit moving ahead.

A useful way to define the problem is to describe the undesirable aspects of the situation.

- Given the previous anecdote from the teacher's viewpoint: "He has difficulty staying in his seat. He constantly is *playing*. He doesn't pay attention." (The teacher is probably a Believer describing a Funster's behavior, with the teacher having little Funster energy or in distress so that she cannot access her Funster floor.)
- From the student's perspective: "She didn't give me time to finish. I couldn't get my pencil sharpened. The directions weren't clear." (This student has probably had all he can take of seatwork. He needs something more expressive and kinesthetic. He is into the second-degree distress of *blaming*.)

If the teacher is unable to see the situation from the student's perspective, it is unlikely that she will be able to define the problem any better. As principal, you might reflect your understanding of the situation: "You're frustrated that he can't stay in his seat and seems to want to play more than work." If you get, "Yes. That's it," then you have reflected what you have been told—understood the situation from the teacher's point of view. If you get, "Not quite," then you may have to restate your understanding in other ways or ask for more information.

Here you might also offer her (privately): "Were there other things that happened before the student's behavior was unacceptable to you?" This approach invites the teacher to consider other things without the principal's accepting ownership of the situation.

### Secure Additional Necessary Information

We are often confronted with limited versions of the situation: People hear what they want to hear and report the version they want known. Adults are no more immune to this selective disclosure than are children.

When staff members cannot solve their problems and become frustrated, they look for allies or rescuers. One way to recruit an ally is to find someone who will agree with us and our perspective. This agreement may come from our position or alliance within the organization for a common purpose or because we know our viewpoints match. As we fashion or reconfirm our alliance, we present the most positive information that invites others to see our position as tenable. That is, we say the things that put us in a favorable light and avoid description of things that may give us a negative pall.

In any event, most administrators are arbiters of what others lay at our feet. We rarely have an opportunity to observe situations unfolding firsthand.

One way to stay apprised is to be out and about during the workday, seeing the programs in operation—management by wandering around (Peters and Austin 1985). In this way, you are familiar with what is happening and the people involved. (If you know folks by their names, they cannot be anonymous in your interactions with them.)

### Determine the Urgency

"Failure to plan on your part does not constitute an emergency on my part!" is a placard or bumper sticker that might be displayed by someone who does not want others intruding needlessly. Another message that indicates failure to plan adequately is, "If I wanted it tomorrow, I'd have asked for it tomorrow."

Sometimes things become urgent for others, and they want our help immediately. Issues of *their* highest priority are presented to us with the expectation that we will see them with the same urgency. The problems of other people may or may not have the same priority for us. We have to assess what else in our schedule may need more immediate attention, or we have to decide to put aside our priorities in deference to others. Of course, this means our work is postponed, and we may become frustrated or angry about having to work later or longer because of the interruption.

This often may be the case in educational situations. Leaders are challenged to assess their priorities constantly. Much of their interaction with others is initiated by others; hence, they may not truly be in control of their priorities.

Even if you have an open-door policy for addressing issues, close the door occasionally. Keep your door open only if you are "open." When you cannot be interrupted, do not allow others to intrude. The more you rescue, the more people will come to you with their "emergencies." Be very careful of responding, "I'll take care of it." No one knows better than you what you can and cannot do—and are willing to do.

## ADAPTING

### Examine Alternatives

With our experience, we develop patterns of dealing with similar issues. When we find something (a "tool") that works, we tend to use it again. Effective problem solving involves determining an appropriate approach for the current situation. (Again, having more tools at your disposal will give you a greater chance of selecting the right one.)

The amount of time we have to address a problem or issue may affect the resources we have to look at various options. Someone said to me once, "It's not an option if I will not do it." If we rush to judgment, we may overlook other viable possibilities.

Another factor that may interfere with our examining options is that we (mostly the Thinkers and Believers among us) tend to look only at the negative consequences. It is important to look at the positive aspects of possibilities, too.

Looking at both celebrating the birthday and attending the professional meeting, we can see the following consequences:

- Positives
  - Fulfill professional expectations
  - Celebrate with child at a convenient time
- Negatives
  - May miss actual celebration
  - May disappoint child by not being at the actual party

With ample time, we can look at a number of possibilities. The number increases with the number of people involved and the permission we give ourselves to "color outside the lines" or "think outside the box."

(Those who may be "locked" into patterns may want to refer to other ways of conceptualizing [De Bono 1970, 1985; Adams 1986]. Also, it is important to note here that breaking away from established patterns is not only for Funsters. We all have the ability to be creative. However, some of us may have difficulty giving ourselves permission to consider other than established patterns or rules.)

Generating ideas can be done in a number of ways. Determining which method works best in a given situation depends on whether we are in the same place (colocated) at the same time (synchronously) or elsewhere (distant) at different times (asynchronously). With current computer software (e.g., Groupware), we can work together synchronously or asynchronously, either at the same site or different locations. There are advantages and disadvantages to each method.

Working in the same location at the same time allows us to interpret the subtle body language we convey when we interact. This collaboration is limited by the people who can meet at a mutual location.

Using current technology allows us to branch out and involve people, regardless of where they are located. They can also respond at different times convenient to their schedules. What is missing, even with interactive televised exchanges, is the nonverbal "language" that helps with our understanding of what others convey. (See Bull 1983; Fast 1970; Hall 1959, 1966; and Mehrabian 1971, 1972 for a more complete discussion of nonverbal language.)

Generating as many ideas as possible is useful if we have sufficient time to examine all of them. One *brainstorming* technique suggests we delay evaluation until all the ideas are presented. Using "author" anonymity permits us to assess the possibilities without attributing the preconceptions we may have about the people who suggest various ways to proceed. (This can be done electronically or by hand, using written ideas that are collated, summarized, and redistributed to the group.)

### Decide on the Approach

Once we are satisfied that we have enough ideas, we can look at the pros and cons of each. We can balance the benefits and calculate the contingencies. Force-field analysis (Lewin 1948) or other techniques can provide the structure for looking at alternatives by examining the *helping* and *hindering* forces. What we are looking for is the best alternative given the current circumstances of the situation.

There is no magic here. What may have worked at another time may not be appropriate now. In many situations, the wisdom of the group may work better than the decision of one individual. Of course, this means that the group has the experience and knowledge to contribute and that the leader is willing to accept what the group offers. The leader may work either as a part of the group or as a supporter of a decision delegated to the group. (For greater depth on situational leadership, see Hersey, Blanchard, and Johnson 1996.)

When group participation is inappropriate (because of compressed time or inexperienced group members), the leader must decide. Here, the leader's experience and knowledge is critical. Insufficient knowledge or unrelated experience will limit the options and the eventual decision.

One technique involving the group would be to classify the generated alternatives as *essential, desirable,* or *possible but impractical.* Codifying each type (5 for essential [E], 3 for desirable [D], and 1 for possible [P]) will facilitate categorizing the possibilities. Once that occurs, *advocacy* of any and all alternatives can proceed. Group members may want to say why one option will or will not work.

If we set a total of 12 (an average of *desirable* for all participants), then we can begin discussion/advocacy on alternatives A, B, D, and E. These all averaged "desirable" or better by the people in the group (as seen in table 11.1).

When advocacy dwindles because of preestablished time limits or loss of energy, we can ask the group to list their top four possibilities. Again, codifying may give us a tool for coalescing opinions (4 for the top choice,

**Table 11.1    Establishing Priorities**

|              | Person 1 | Person 2 | Person 3 | Person 4 | Total |
|--------------|----------|----------|----------|----------|-------|
| Alternative A | E | P | D | E | 14 |
| Alternative B | E | D | D | E | 16 |
| Alternative C | P | D | D | P | 8 |
| Alternative D | E | D | E | E | 18 |
| Alternative E | D | E | D | D | 14 |

3 for the second favorite, 2 for the third favorite, and 1 for the fourth favorite). From there, sums can be tallied, and the group can see the collective choice—the one with the highest total. See table 11.2. (Note: Each rank may be used only once. No ties should be allowed.)

Alternative B has the strongest support and should be the highest priority. If there are no mitigating circumstances (such as legal or budgetary considerations), then alternative B should be implemented. If we are looking at our long-term goals and more than one can be addressed, then alternative B is followed by A, C, and D, in that order. If B will not work for some reason (e.g., it is too costly), even though it seems to be the best solution, then A would be the next best solution to be implemented.

## COMMUNICATING

### Develop a Plan

The preferred alternative provides the direction for addressing the identified problem. The development of an implementation plan is—and should be—left to those who are charged with addressing the problem directly. Ownership of implementation specifics invests the stakeholders in the outcomes.

It is here that understanding interaction style preferences becomes important. Each of us has a preference for a particular style—*autocratic, democratic, benevolent,* or *laissez-faire* (presented in detail in chapter 3 and discussed further in the epilogue). Adopting an *individualistic* style (Kahler 1982) gives one the full range of tools with which to work.

The leader who is energized and can go to the appropriate floor is

**Table 11.2  Choosing among Alternatives**

|  | *Person 1* | *Person 2* | *Person 3* | *Person 4* | *Total* |
|---|---|---|---|---|---|
| Alternative A | 4 | 3 | 3 | 1 | 11 |
| Alternative B | 3 | 4 | 4 | 2 | 13 |
| Alternative D | 2 | 2 | 2 | 4 | 10 |
| Alternative E | 1 | 1 | 1 | 3 | 6 |

able deal with others effectively. He or she will interact with Doers and Dreamers autocratically, with Thinkers and Believers democratically, with Feelers benevolently, and with Funsters in a laissez-faire manner. Interestingly, each of the other different people will respond positively with this approach if we communicate in the appropriate channel and use another's perceptual preference.

The drawbacks or shortcomings are apparent when we do not get our own needs met and cannot get on our "elevator," or if one or more of our "floors" is not furnished well enough for us to stay there for the period of time our colleagues may need or prefer. Those are the times when we go to where *we* are most comfortable and familiar. If others accept our invitation to be there too, we will be effective. If they reject the invitation, we will have to find another *venue* or postpone the interaction until we are more motivated (having met our individual needs).

If we have sufficient energy to *shift*, we can accommodate the preferences of others. The following examples reflect shifting (note the channels and perceptions in table 11.3):

- To a Feeler's perspective: "Barbara, you are very sensitive to this issue. How might we all work with each other?" (Nurturative channel, focusing on feelings)
- To a Thinker's perspective: "Alfred, you always have such good ideas. What do you think our options are?" (Requestive channel, focusing on thoughts)
- To a Believer's Perspective: "Matthew, this is a very important project. What do you believe the right approach is?" (Requestive channel, focusing on opinions)

**Table 11.3  Personalities and Communication Channels**

| Personality | Interaction Style | Channel | Perception |
|---|---|---|---|
| Feeler | Benevolent | Nurturative | Emotions |
| Thinker | Democratic | Requestive | Thoughts |
| Believer | Democratic | Requestive | Beliefs |
| Dreamer | Autocratic | Directive | Reflections |
| Funster | Laissez Faire | Emotive | Reactions |
| Doer | Autocratic | Directive | Actions |

(Adapted with permission from Kahler [1982, 1996].)

- To a Dreamer's perspective: "Dorothy, tell me how you imagine the path we agreed to take." (Directive channel, focusing on reflections)
- To a Funster's perspective: "Angie, what a great opportunity for your creative juices! Give me some of the super ideas you like by next Tuesday." (Emotive channel, focusing on reactions)
- To a Doer's perspective: "Doug, you're the man (for the job). Come up with an approach so we can get the job done." (Directive channel, focusing on action)

For most educators, communicating with Barbara, Alfred, and Matthew will be most comfortable and familiar. Dorothy, Angie, and Doug may take a little to a lot more effort. For some of us, Angie and Doug are too difficult, and we will invite them elsewhere on a fairly regular basis. If they do not/cannot accept the invitation, we may have laid the groundwork for ongoing miscommunication, leading to continual conflict.

Ongoing rejection of communication invitations can lead to a predictable pattern, a *dance*—an interaction with a cadence but lack of progress:

- Matthew (Believer): "Why don't you start with polling the faculty for their ideas?"
- Angie (Funster): "Yeah, that might be a good way to start, but I am not sure they will like having to give up their free time."
- Matthew: "Well, why don't ask them for the times when they are available to work with you?"
- Angie: "That might work, but I would need to spend time with them explaining the project."
- Matthew: "Why don't you . . . ?"
- Angie: "Yes, but . . ."
- Matthew: "Why don't you . . . ?"
- Angie: "Yes, but . . ."

You can hear the "beat" and see the lack of progress. When these two people leave the interaction with nothing really accomplished, Matthew might say to himself: "What is it with Angie? Is she so dense that she can't see how important this project is? Why do I have to explain every-thing to her?"

Angie's reaction might be: "I don't like this project. I don't like Mat-thew's constantly trying to get me to take over. I don't want to do it. Anyway, he hasn't given me all the resources I need."

### How Do You Know?

Trying to see a situation from another person's perspective indicates (1) you are willing to put aside your preferences for a time, and (2) you understand another's preferences and motivation.

Process Communication gives us the tools to interpret preferences and motivation through the words, tones, postures, gestures, and facial expression people use. (Another way of determining one's preferences and motivation is through a profile generated from responses to an inventory.) The predictable patterns of distress behaviors (table 11.4) tell us what people want and what drives them. If we listen to the words that people use, we can understand their perceptual preferences and move to the appropriate channel.

**Table 11.4   Distress Patterns, Conflict Style, and Masks**

| Personality | First Degree | Second Degree | Conflict Mgt. | Mask |
|---|---|---|---|---|
| Feeler | Overadapts | Invites criticism | Avoidance; Suppression | Drooper (I'm not OK) |
| Thinker | Does not delegate | Overcontrols | Domination; Compromise | Attacker (You're not OK) |
| Believer | Focuses negatively | Pushes beliefs | Domination; Compromise | Attacker (You're not OK) |
| Dreamer | Does not finalize | Withdraws | Avoidance | Drooper (I'm not OK) |
| Funster | Delegates inappropriately | Blames | Suppression; Domination | Blamer (You're not OK) |
| Doer | Does not support | Manipulates | Suppression; Domination | Blamer (You're not OK) |

[Adapted with permission from Kahler, T. (1982), and Kahler, T. (1996).]

## Implement the Decision

Once the plan of operation is determined, key staff will implement the plan. Again, if those who are charged with the implementation have contributed to the decision, they are likely to be more enthusiastic about how well it is implemented. Owners of the decision are more invested in its positive outcomes. That is, if I help to make a decision, I want it to work well.

## Determine the Success

Administrators often look to their titular authority and assume their decision has been implemented and has been effective because they made the decision. To verify their authority, they should move past the assumption that organizational status is sufficient to cause action. It is more realistic to look to the compliance and enthusiasm of staff.

Further, it is important to assess if the decision is effective. Just because a decision has been made does not mean it will accomplish the planned outcome.

If we set out in a given direction knowing it will take a certain amount of time to get where we are going, we need to check our progress periodically. Preestablishing benchmarks or checkpoints is a useful way to see if we are headed in the right direction and are making steady progress.

If our goal is Memphis and we head west on Interstate 40 from Nashville, we should "achieve" Memphis (about 200 miles away) in about three hours. If we drive the speed limit and there are no detours or traffic clogs, what do we do if there is "no" Memphis in four hours? Do we continue driving? (Of course not, but some might continue.) Do we stop and ask for directions? (Not a bad idea!) Do we check our progress? (A really good option.)

With educational programs, we see some inertia. Movement causes further movement—whether or not there are reasons to check if the movement is productive. Conversely, lack of movement tends to perpetuate no movement; that is, nothing changes without great effort. (This is very similar to the physical law that says a body in motion tends to stay in motion, and a body at rest tends to stay at rest unless acted upon by an outside force.)

Effective educational leaders are the forces to stimulate change—encouraging people to go places they would not choose by themselves (Barker 1999). It is important to be sure the signposts are in place before we set out. We need to specify our indicators for success as we put our plan in operation and look to those indicators as the program unfolds, making adjustments as necessary. This is *task focus*.

A sometimes-lost but equally important component is whether the people involved in a project are satisfied—whether their morale is high enough to keep them motivated to the benefit of the organization (and for themselves). This *relationship focus* when combined with *task focus* yields the potential for *individualistic leadership* (the opportunity to express high degrees of concern for both outcomes and the satisfaction that leads to high morale).

The Process Communication Model gives us the interaction *signposts* for success. If we know what the signals of distress (unfulfilled need) are, we can make appropriate adjustments in our style (if the distress is related to the project). Distress in one's personal life can interfere, but leaders should be cautious about trespassing without permission into the lives of their colleagues.

For example, if you see the patterns shown in table 11.5, with what type of person are you interacting and what might you do professionally? (A formula you might use is to deal with the behavior first, then try to find the appropriate channel and perception to *communicate*—to reach understanding. See appendix D for the personality types and suggestions for assisting each to stay energized and stay out of distress.)

**Table 11.5   Activity**

|                     | Personality Type | Invitation |
| ------------------- | ---------------- | ---------- |
| Withdraws           |                  |            |
| Overcontrols        |                  |            |
| Becomes vindictive  |                  |            |
| Preaches            |                  |            |
| Blames              |                  |            |
| Invites criticism   |                  |            |

(Adapted with permission from Kahler [1982].)

People in distress are not as open to communication as those who are motivated—that is, unfulfilled needs motivate a person to focus on fulfilling those needs, mostly with negative behaviors. As our energy is channeled to getting our needs met, we have little energy to focus on what others may need. We cannot *shift* to other frames of preference (see appendix A) until our own needs are satisfied, and until we regenerate the energy to be motivated to look beyond ourselves. Knowing negative behaviors allows a leader to understand what others are experiencing and to interact with them in meaningful ways.

Table 11.6 encapsulates the frames of preference for the personality phases educational leaders are likely to see in colleagues, students, and others in their professional (and personal) lives. These *frames* provide indicators for distress and suggestions for both intervening in distress and for preventing distress. (A more extensive list is found in appendix A.)

Your effectiveness as an educational leader will be found in your ability to communicate—the degree to which you are able to get others to understand your perspective and message. Further, your leadership will be measured by your ability to guide others to places they would not choose by themselves.

## POINTS TO PONDER

- The causes or sources of conflict should be diagnosed carefully.
- In dealing with conflict, effective leaders need to adapt the way they see things.
- They need to *shift* to the preferences of the parties in conflict to communicate effectively.

## REFERENCES

Adams, J. L. 1986. *Conceptual blockbusting: A guide to better ideas.* 3rd ed. Reading, Mass.: Addison-Wesley.

Barker, J. L. 1999. *Leadershift: Five lessons for leaders in the twenty-first century.* St. Paul, Minn.: Star Thrower Productions (video).

**Table 11.6 Frames of Preference**

| Type | Feeler | Thinker | Believer | Dreamer | Funster | Doer |
|---|---|---|---|---|---|---|
| Strengths | Compassionate, sensitive, warm | Logical, responsible, organized | Conscientious, dedicated, observant | Imaginative, reflective, calm | Spontaneous, creative, playful | Adaptable, persuasive, charming |
| Perceptions | Feelings | Thoughts | Beliefs | Reflections (inactions) | Reactions (likes & dislikes) | Actions |
| Needs | Acceptance of self; sensory stimuli | Recognition of work; time structure | Recognition of work; convictions | Solitude | Contact | Incidence |
| First-Degree Distress | Wants to please others; overadapts | Expects perfect self; overthinks for others | Expects perfect others; focuses on what's wrong | Has to be strong to survive | Tries harder; feigns lack of understanding | Expects others to be strong |
| Second-Degree Distress | Appears confused; makes mistakes; invites others to criticize | Critical about time, fairness, responsibility issues | Preaches, crusades, critical about details | Withdraws; is embarrassed; overly shy | Blames others; acts irresponsibly; invites negative sanctions | Manipulates; break rules; sets up negative drama |
| Intervention | Nurture, stroke verbally | Clarify issues; provide facts/data | Acknowledge beliefs; recognize value of work | Allow private time/own space; direct to action | Interact playfully, with high energy | Focus on exciting ways of doing things; provide lots of activity |
| Prevention | Comfortable workplace; group activities; personal connection | Clear time frame; rewards for accomplishments | Obvious rules & structure; projects that appeal to belief system | Projects to be done alone; permission to withdraw; limited group activities | Playful contact; acceptance of play before work | Short-term assignments; positive competition; physical involvement |

[Adapted with permission from Kahler, T. (1982), and Kahler, T. (1996).]

Barnard, C. I. 1938. *The functions of the executive*. Cambridge, Mass.: Harvard University Press.

Blake, R. R., and J. S. Mouton. 1985. *The managerial grid III: A new look at the classic that has boosted productivity and profits for thousands of corporations worldwide*. Houston: Gulf Publishing.

Bolton, R. 1979. *People skills: How to assert yourself, listen to others, and resolve conflicts*. Englewood Cliffs, N.J.: Prentice-Hall.

Bull, P. 1983. *Body movement and interpersonal communication*. New York: Wiley.

De Bono, E. 1985. *Six thinking hats*. Toronto: Little, Brown and Co.

Fast, J. 1970. *Body language*. New York: Pocket Books.

Gamble, T. K., and M. Gamble. 1982. *Contacts: Communicating interpersonally*. New York: Random House.

Glatthorn, A. A., and H. R. Adams. 1983. *Listening your way to management success*. Glenview, Ill.: Scott, Foresman.

Hall, E. T. 1959. *The silent language*. Garden City, N.Y.: Doubleday.

———. 1966. *The hidden dimension*. Garden City, N.Y.: Doubleday.

Hersey, P., K. Blanchard, and D. E. Johnson. 1996. *Management of organizational behavior: Utilizing human resources*. 7th ed. Englewood Cliffs, N.J.: Prentice-Hall.

Kahler, T. 1982. *Personality pattern inventory validation studies*. Little Rock, Ark.: Kahler Communications.

———. 1995. *The process teaching seminar*. Little Rock, Ark.: Kahler Communications.

———. 1996. *Key to me for students profile*. Little Rock, Ark.: Kahler Communications.

Lewin, K. 1948. *Resolving social conflicts: Selected papers on group dynamics*. Edited by G. W. Lewin. New York: Harper.

Maurer, R. E. 1991. *Managing conflict: Tactics for school administrators*. Needham Heights, Mass.: Allyn and Bacon.

Mehrabian, A. 1971. *Silent messages*. Belmont, Calif.: Wadsworth Publishing.

———. 1972. *Nonverbal communication*. Chicago: Aldine-Atherton.

Metcalf, H. C., and L. Urwick, (eds.). 1940. *Dynamic administration: The collected papers of Mary Parker Follett*. New York: Harper and Row.

Ouchi, W. G. 1982. *Theory Z: How American business can meet the Japanese challenge*. New York: Avon.

Peters, T., and N. Austin. 1985. *A passion for excellence: The leadership difference*. New York: Random House.

# Epilogue

## Installing the Capstones

Inspecting the finished product and making necessary adjustments are benchmarks of effective builders. If the joints are misaligned or there are paint spatters, it is important that the builder modify the work to a higher standard.

As an educational leader, you might do similar inspections. Following an interaction, you might ask:

- What was the objective of the meeting?
- Did we accomplish the objective?
  - What techniques helped in accomplishing the objective?
  - What barriers did we fail to overcome?
- What might we have done differently to achieve a better result?

Affirming what worked well and changing what did not are important aftermaths. Many want to focus only on the negative results, and others want to avoid analyzing altogether. Acknowledging what has worked is a key to giving yourself well-earned credit and reinforcing effective leadership.

Drawing on the tools and techniques of Process Communication, we can use an Assessing Matrix (Kahler 1982). In figure E.1 we see that each personality type falls into one of four quadrants (remembering that we are a composite of all personalities). One axis describes how we interact, from Involved to Withdrawn; the other axis describes the degree to which we are motivated intrinsically or extrinsically.

We see that the personality types most associated with educators

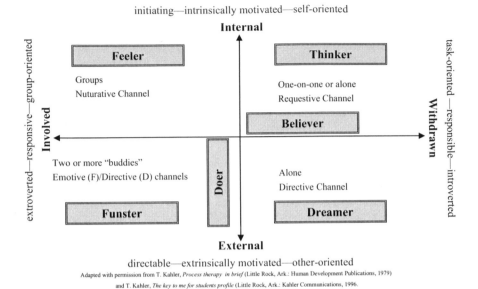

**Figure E.1   Assessing Matrix**


(Feeler, Thinker, and Believer) are motivated from within with varying
degrees of involvement. Those who prefer to be more involved (Feelers) enjoy the company of others and prefer to work in groups. Those
who prefer less involvement (Thinkers and Believers) would rather interact either one on one or alone.

Those who prefer to be less involved with others tend to be more *task
oriented.* Conversely, those who prefer greater involvement are more
*relationship oriented.*

The challenge for most educators is *shifting* to where they can interact effectively with those (Dreamer, Funster, and Doer) who need external motivation—a quality not very common in educators. However,
many educators may have sparsely furnished "floors" where they might
interact with those who prefer external motivation. That is, the tools
available on those floors are simple. Not used very often by educators,
they may feel awkward in the hands of those preferring more familiar
techniques.

Below is a situation we might use as a capstone (a component that
completes the roof of a building and makes it sound) to the communication and interaction framework discussed above. A large district had re-

roofed a school one year, and it leaked after the first serious rain after the project was completed. The contract had gone to the lowest bidder, and the contractor had neglected to install capstones. (The installation was neither specified in the contract, nor did the contractor follow an industry standard.) It was an important lesson: Capstones are crucial if roofs are to be sound—and the lowest bidder is not necessarily the best.

The following vignette is an example of a problem that might arise in a school. Although it might seem simple or something that is unlikely to happen, problems like these do occur.

> You are the principal of a middle school of 900 pupils. The community is supportive of the school and of you as its administrator. One of your students has refused to obey one of the teachers. The student would not do the class work in ink, as required by the teacher; instead, the work was done in pencil, even though the student had a pen. The teacher sent the student to you for being insubordinate. You have asked the teacher, the student, and the student's parent to meet with you.

The parent is very busy and seems agitated at interrupting the workday to attend a meeting at school. The student is the middle of three children, ages seventeen, fourteen, and eleven. They are all good students.

The teacher has a very orderly classroom. The chairs are in neat rows; students have assigned seats; and there are specific guidelines for how class work is to be done. The teacher insists on strict compliance with classroom guidelines because of the belief that it promotes good discipline in the students. They respond by doing neat and precise work. They also perform at above-average levels on district and statewide tests.

The student preferred to write in pencil because a mistake can be erased. The teacher has refused to accept the latest assignment because it is in pencil. The teacher will not yield to the explanation that it is more convenient to be able to erase when mistakes are made rather than to start over.

How might you deal with this situation to resolve the problem(s)? Of course, first decide whose "monkey" it is.

The teacher is upset because the rules were broken. The parent does not want to interrupt the workday. The student wants special treatment.

None of these people can *resolve* the situation by or among themselves and need your assistance.

If you were Dorothy (the Dreamer) or Doug (the Doer), you would most likely take an *autocratic* (directive) approach. However, Dorothy might try to avoid a confrontation unless she could *shift* to some other part of her personality. She would be uncomfortable with everyone in distress and having the prospect of dealing with them face to face.

> Doug/Dorothy: "I understand that Teacher has classroom guidelines. They seem reasonable, and students are obliged to follow reasonable rules and directives.
> "Parent, please assist us by telling your child that rules are meant to be followed.
> "Student, follow Teacher's rules.
> "Teacher, tell me if there are other things we need to do."

This matter-of-fact approach encourages others to respond directly. It works best with those who require direction, structure, or training. It does not encourage group interaction or feedback. It invites rebellious behavior.

The directive nature will probably upset the parent further. The parent may respond in one of two ways: "Why do I need to be here? A phone call or a note could have accomplished the same thing." Or "How dare you tell me what to do? Just who do you think you are?" This will set up a battle with the parent either way.

The student is likely to feel disengaged and powerless: (1) "They never listen to me. Why bother? I am always wrong." Or (2) "OK! If that's the way it is, I'll do it, but I'll get them—all of them—some other way."

The student may seem to comply, but the perceived incompatibility— the conflict—has not been resolved. As a result, the conflict is likely to resurface in other ways.

If you were Matthew (the Believer) or Alfred (the Thinker), you would take a *democratic* approach. However, you would find it important to emphasize the rules or that the student do what is right or expected.

Matthew/Alfred: "I understand we have a problem with Student's not following how Teacher expects assignments to be done.

"Teacher, will you explain your classroom guidelines and why they are
important?

"Student, will you listen carefully and ask questions about anything you
do not understand?

"Parent, will you support us?"

The *democratic* administrator attempts to involve all the participants.
He or she encourages them to be goal oriented. In this case, the goal of
the teacher and the focus of the administrator is that students comply
with the rules. However, this approach does not allow students to di-
verge from the rules, or accommodate those who may not understand
their responsibilities or who may be unwilling to comply. The teacher's
rules will be reinforced (but may be brought into question).

The parent may still be confused or upset at the intrusion into the
workday: "I am not exactly sure why they needed me here just to ask
me to support their rules. They could have done it over the telephone
or in a note."

The student may get into a *try hard* position: "Well, if Teacher had
explained it better, I would have done the work differently." Or engage
in "Yes, but . . .": "I understand the rules, but when I make mistakes, I
would rather erase them than start over."

If you were Barbara (the Feeler), you would attempt to be highly empathic with everyone. You want harmony and would choose a *benevolent*
approach.

Barbara: "I see we seem to have a problem. Let's see if we can work
something out where everyone will be happy.

"Student, you know things would be OK, if you would just follow Teacher's rules."

"Parent, I am sure you can help Student to understand how to get along
in Teacher's class."

"Teacher, might there be a way to accept Student's work this time, if
there is a promise to follow the rules in the future?"

This approach focuses on people and attempts to resolve problems
in a nurturing and accepting way. It works well with people who are

predominantly feeling oriented and who need unconditional acceptance. It is disadvantageous if the task is ignored. That is, people may *feel* better, but the problem may only be suppressed or ignored.

The student may feel patronized, and the issue of using a pencil has not been addressed, other than an allusion to following the rules in the future. The student might say, "Yeah, I guess I can do that," but might not stick to the "agreement."

The parent has not been engaged in the solution, but has been directed, albeit gently, to support the school. The situation has been avoided. "Excuse me," the parent might say. "Can we talk about the problem here?"

Without unconditional support for the classroom rules, the teacher might feel discounted. "No, I will not accept Student's work. The rules were known from the first day. They are posted in the classroom, and students acknowledged they understood them during class orientation."

The *benevolent* approach may have inflamed the situation. The problem has not been resolved.

If you were Angie (the Funster), you would take a *laissez-faire* approach. You would be nondirective and want the participants to accept responsibility for resolving the problem.

> Angie: "Well, Student, I hear you have a problem.
> "Teacher, you don't really need my help . . . now do you?
> "Parent, thanks for comin' in. I know you can help."

This detached attitude will have everyone doing some serious head scratching—wondering about the purpose of the meeting and what the direction is. The *laissez-faire* approach works well for individuals who can and are willing to accept responsibility for their actions; it invites independence and creativity. It does not, however, provide direction for people who need structure and guidance.

The student might think: "Well, yeah, I have a problem. What do you think I'm doin' here?"

The teacher may stay silent and acknowledge: "Well, yes. I suppose I can handle it." Or the teacher may reassert the frustration that prompted the meeting: "Yes, I do need your help. I have tried all I know how to do." And may even become argumentative: "Why do you think I came here in the first place?"

The parent may try to redirect the administrator and seek more information: "Precisely what is it that you would recommend I do?"

Again, the problem is not resolved. In fact, another layer may have been added—lack of communication.

If communication is understanding a message in the way the sender intended and responding appropriately, we might consider the *individualistic* approach (see chapter 3) to the situation. This requires a person to *shift* to a different style when necessary. Moreover, it requires that we consider *how* we communicate, as well as *what* we communicate (Kahler 1982).

Of course, we want others to own the problem and participate in the resolution. As we look at a possible scenario, we want to be sure to act as a facilitator rather than appearing to be all-knowing or accepting the problem as ours.

Most administrators will begin to define a problem by turning first to the one who presents the need for resolution. Another way to proceed is to start with the person with the least amount of power (if that is a different person).

Shifter: "Student, can you tell me why you are here?"
Student: "I dunno. Teacher's pickin' on me."
Shifter: "Teacher doesn't understand what you are saying."
Student: "Yeah . . . but I can't do my work the way I want."
Shifter: "Would there be a problem if you could do your work your way?"
Student: "Nope."

The administrator has reflected that she understands what the student has said. Nothing has been done yet to resolve the situation. Given that the student has been understood, it is likely he will be engaged in the eventual resolution—at least, he has not been discounted or discarded from the process.

Many times administrators presume the student is wrong; otherwise, why would the teacher have brought the student in the first place? That approach does little more than exclude the student from the outset. If we want students (or others) to change their behavior, we have to include them in the process or the decision making. Without that involvement, there can be no *integration* or ownership in the final decision.

Shifter: "Parent, what do you see the problem to be?"
Parent: "I'm not sure, but I think it is an issue of following Teacher's rules."
Shifter: "It appears to be the case to me, too"
Parent: "I am not exactly sure how I can help."
Shifter: "Will you help Student follow through on whatever we all decide might be a start?"
Parent: "Oh, I think I can support that."

Asking for the parent's help without being demanding, demeaning, or challenging the parent's authority with the student will go a long way to resolving the situation. If the parent is part of the solution, you may have recruited an ally.

Shifter: "Teacher, as I understand the situation, Student prefers to work in pencil, which is different from your expectations. Is that correct?"
Teacher: "Yes."
Shifter: "Is there anything else that is going on with Student's work?"
Teacher: "Not that I am aware of. The work, itself, is good to excellent."
Shifter: "Other than to enforce your rules and to reiterate them when necessary, have you talked with Student about the lapse?"
Teacher: "Not really. Rules are rules, and these expectations seem reasonable to me. Also, they were discussed when we began the class."
Shifter: "How do you propose to proceed?"
Teacher: "I simply want Student to do the work as expected, with no variation."

Everyone has had a chance to participate, starting with the one with the least amount of power. The administrator has engaged everyone without taking sides or trying to resolve someone else's problem. Everyone seems to agree what the problem is—failure to follow classroom rules.

Shifter: "Everyone seems to agree. The issue is following Teacher's expectations for how work should be done.
"Student, you would prefer to do it your way.
"Parent, you are willing to support what we decide.
"Teacher, you want your rules obeyed.
"So, how might we solve this issue? Student, what is your suggestion?"

Student: "I dunno. Doing my work in ink doesn't let me erase if I need to."

Shifter: "Teacher, do you see another option?"

Teacher: "Well, if erasing is the problem, why not use an erasable pen?"

Shifter: "Hmm! That sounds like a plan. Student, will that work for you?"

Student: "I guess."

Shifter: "You will be able to erase when you need to and still follow Teacher's rules. OK?"

Student: "Yeah."

Shifter: "Parent, is this something you can support?"

Parent: "Sounds good to me."

Shifter: "OK. It is my understanding that Student will submit class work in erasable pen, and that Student will talk with Teacher about any problems as they arise rather than disobeying classroom rules. Is that OK with everyone?"

If you feel any misunderstanding still remains, you may want to write a "memorandum (or letter) of understanding" to all parties to reiterate the agreement. In that way, everyone has a written version of the oral agreement, which may be used should a similar problem arise.

It would seem that the immediate problem has been resolved integratively—both parties (here, the teacher and the student) contributing with neither party losing. Since no one has lost, the situation is unlikely to reemerge. It is a win-win solution, or resolution: the teacher's rules remain intact; the student can erase when necessary; and the parent has been involved in the student's support.

Not all problems can be resolved creatively or integratively, and attempting to use *integration* takes longer. Resolving problems integratively, however, is longer lasting (perhaps, even permanent) than ignoring, suppressing, dominating, or compromising.

## POINTS TO PONDER

- Each of us has preferred ways of doing things, of handling conflicts in specific ways.
- If everyone involved in a conflict sees things in the same way and communicates similarly, then resolving the conflict moves more

easily; if perceptual and communication styles are different, broaching the conflict is more problematic.

- Understanding the differences gives a leader clues as to how to communicate effectively.
- *Shifting* into other *frames of preference* is the key to effective conflict resolution.

## REFERENCES

Kahler, T. 1979. *Process therapy in brief*. Little Rock, Ark.: Human Development Publications.

———. 1982. *Process communication management seminar*. Little Rock, Ark.: Kahler Communications.

———. 1996. *Key to me for students profile*. Little Rock, Ark.: Kahler Communications.

# APPENDIX A

## Frames of Preference

Presented in this section you will find a review of the character strengths, perceptual preferences, main motivators, and distress patterns for each of the personality types you encountered earlier. Also included are extended lists of suggestions for each personality to keep batteries charged and remain energized. For you, the list suggests how you can stay in a place where you are motivated. For others whose personalities and needs you understand, the lists give you ways you can connect with them, intervene in their distress, and suggest to them ways in which they can stay energized and motivated. (Adapted with permission from T. Kahler, *The process teaching seminar* [Little Rock, Ark.: Kahler Communications, 1995] and T. Kahler, *Key to me for students profile* [Little Rock, Ark.: Kahler Communications, 1996].)

## FEELER

| | |
|---|---|
| Character Strengths: | Compassionate, sensitive, warm |
| Perceptual Preferences: | Feelings, emotions, sensations |
| Motivating Factors: | Personal attention/appreciation; sensory satisfaction |
| Distress Patterns: | |
| First Degree: | Wants to please others; overadapts to people/ situations |
| Second Degree: | Appears confused; makes mistakes; invites criticism |
| Needs Fulfillment: | Creating own "nest" at home and work |
| | Arranging for personal recognition and acceptance |
| | Working with groups of people who appreciate you |
| | Volunteering for projects that help others |
| | Spending special time with children (yours or others) |
| | Getting massage or back rub |
| | Keeping fresh flowers available to be seen and smelled |
| | Having special pictures of loved ones to be seen by self and others |
| | Using incense, aromatic candles, and/or potpourri |
| | Taking bubble baths |
| | Having lunch with a close friend/spouse regularly |
| | Using best china, linen, and silver without need of special occasion |
| | Strolling through fragrance section of department store |
| | Buying your favorite cologne/scent |
| | Telling and receiving messages of "I love you!" |
| | Giving and receiving hugs |
| | Walking in the garden, forest, rain, and so forth |
| | "Dressing" for dinner |

## THINKER

| | |
|---|---|
| Character Strengths: | Logical, responsible, organized |
| Perceptual Preferences: | Thoughts, ideas, facts, information |
| Motivating Factors: | Recognition for work; time structure |
| Distress Patterns: | |
| First Degree: | Wants to be perfect; overcontrols; delegates poorly or not at all |
| Second Degree: | Becomes critical about fairness, responsibility, time; attacks others who do not think clearly |
| Needs Fulfillment: | Setting priorities |

Focusing on doing what is most important

Arranging for acknowledgment of accomplishments

Having clear times frames and responsibilities

Making "to do" lists and crossing off what has been completed

Keeping a journal

Using an appointment book/calendar

Displaying tangible recognition of work—certificates, plaques, and so on

Creating awards for family for accomplished tasks/responsibilities

Taking on tasks with tangible outcomes of completion

Attending workshop to increase skill or expertise/data base

Having a hobby with tangible outcomes—gardening or similar activities

Rewarding self with "Certificate of Accomplishment"

Having a trusted "sounding board" for ideas or proposed projects

## BELIEVER

| | |
|---|---|
| Character Strengths: | Conscientious, dedicated, observant |
| Perceptual Preferences: | Beliefs, opinions, values |
| Motivating Factors: | Recognition for work; acceptance of convictions |
| Distress Patterns: | |
| First Degree: | Wants others to be perfect; focuses on what is wrong |
| Second Degree: | Frustrated with differing opinions; preaches/ crusades about things of perceived importance; is suspicious; criticizes details and lack of commitment |
| Needs Fulfillment: | Joining/increasing religious activities/ affiliations |

Discussing religion, politics, and current events

Sharing personal values and beliefs with trusted colleagues

Contributing time/money to worthy cause

Involving family in community-based activities

Establishing rules, structure, procedures for projects

Proposing/implementing projects that affirm belief system

Campaigning on behalf of candidate/important issue

Mentoring a colleague, supervisee, or less experienced person

Listing (and framing) "My Ten Most Important Values"

Displaying saying or idea supporting beliefs

Sharing opinions with colleagues about what works well for you

"Practicing what you preach"

Being assertive about your limits

Writing a letter to the editor

## DREAMER

| | |
|---|---|
| Character Strengths: | Imaginative, reflective, calm |
| Perceptual Preferences: | Reflections; inactions |
| Motivating Factors: | Solitude; personal space |
| Distress Patterns: | |
| First Degree: | Needs to be strong |
| Second Degree: | Appears embarrassed; is shy; withdraws |
| Needs Fulfillment: | Spending alone time |

Volunteering for projects to be done alone

Meditating

Taking up solitary pursuits—cycling, walking, and so on

Taking vacations alone

Collecting coins, stamps, and similar activities

Closing the office door when things are too active

Reading

Receiving clear directions, then being left alone

Having office/work place out of the mainstream

Collecting data/doing "quiet" research (library, etc.)

Establishing routines for repetitive tasks

Setting limits for interaction, then withdrawing if they are exceeded

## FUNSTER

| | |
|---|---|
| Character Strengths: | Spontaneous, creative, playful |
| Perceptual Preferences: | Reactions (likes and dislikes) |
| Motivating Factors: | Contact, fun activities |
| Distress Patterns: | |
| First Degree: | Tries hard; feigns lack of understanding/ inability |
| Second Degree: | Blames others; acts irresponsibly; invites negative sanctions |
| Needs Fulfillment: | Having a good sense of humor |

Telling jokes and amusing anecdotes

Using word play and puns

Playing *before* work

Reacting with excitement: "Wow!" "C-ooo-l!"

Playing a musical instrument

Writing music or short stories or plays

Painting, sculpting, or other artistic outlets

Decorating with exciting colors and stimulating things

Being active in sports that are fun

Staying involved in projects with "buddies"

Dressing for the "mood"

Using a "Walkman" while working or exercising

Taking a play break at work—video/computer games or similar activities

Looking for creative solutions to knotty problems

Acting in community theater

"Coloring outside the lines"

## DOER

| | |
|---|---|
| Character Strengths: | Adaptable, persuasive, charming |
| Perceptual Preferences: | Actions |
| Motivating Factors: | Incidence; excitement |
| Distress Patterns: | |
|   First Degree: | Wants others to be strong/fend for themselves |
|   Second Degree: | Attempts to manipulate people/situations; breaks rules; tries to instigate conflict between others |
| Needs Fulfillment: | Having lots of things going on |

Being involved in projects/tasks with quick
   rewards/payoffs

Competing positively

Being involved in physical/kinesthetic things

Getting to the "bottom line"

Getting involved in exciting projects

Negotiating "perks" for tasks completed well
   before deadlines

Traveling on professional business as often as
   possible

Riding the big rides at the fair/amusement
   park

"Playing" the stock market (within monetary
   constraints)

Driving a "fun" car—convertible, five-speed,
   "red"

Dressing to impress others (again, within
   budgetary limits)

# Appendix B

# Listening Effectiveness of Educators

## AN EXAMINATION OF LISTENING EFFECTIVENESS OF EDUCATORS

*Purpose of the Study*

Because listening occupies such a predominant place in most classroom instruction—far in excess of the noninstructional use noted by Rankin, Nichols, Steil, and others (Gilbert 1989)—the purpose of the study was to determine how well educators perform the skill they require most students to use 65 to 90 percent of classroom time.

*Instrumentation*

Listening effectiveness was determined by an overall score on the Watson-Barker Listening Test (WBLT) (Watson and Barker 1995), standardized for adult audiences and divided into five sections: (1) evaluating message content, (2) understanding meaning in conversations, (3) understanding and remembering information, (4) evaluating emotional meanings in messages, and (5) following directions and instructions. The WBLT took approximately twenty minutes to administer in group settings. Data were collected during the summer and fall of 1996.

Several thousand subjects across the United States were used to refine and validate the WBLT, including executives, professionals, government employees, and undergraduate/graduate students from a variety of universities and curricula. Pilot tests were subjected to factor analyses, item analyses, reliability tests, and descriptive analyses. Face validity of each item was judged by a panel of listening experts (Watson and Barker 1995). In addition, Roberts (1986, 1988) and others (as reported in Watson and Barker 1995) reported the WBLT to be valid.

The data used for this research were the overall and subscores on the WBLT. The demographic categories (independent variables) were gender, site, educational level of work (elementary, middle, high, central administrative), and sector (public, private, parochial). Personality designations were derived from Kahler's (1986) Personality Pattern Inventory (PPI).

### Sample

The original research design only included university faculty in a college of professional educator preparation. Because teachers are teachers, regardless of the venue or audience, the decision was made to expand the sample to include professional educators from the precollegiate arena as well. Data were gathered from 322 subjects.

The sample was predominantly female (n = 238, 74 percent) from public (n = 302, 94 percent) high schools (n = 177, 55 percent). The sites included one university, two elementary schools, one middle school, three high schools, one school district, one private school, and principals from a statewide parochial system. All of the subjects worked in Arkansas.

Eighty-nine percent of the group were base Feelers (41 percent), Thinkers (12 percent), and Believers (36 percent), and 74 percent were phase Feelers (21 percent), Thinkers (24 percent), and Believers (29 percent). Two-thirds of the group was either a base Feeler, Thinker, or Believer, with one of these other types as the phase (see table B.2). These data also show this group of educators was 10 percent base Funsters (with no base Doers) and 16 percent phase Funsters (10 percent) or Doers (6 percent). The comparative data between the general population and the research sample are shown in table B.1. (Note: Not all of the subjects completed both the PPI and the WBLT.)

It was interesting to note that none of the sample group of educators was Doer-based—that is, no one who chose education did so from a

**Table B.1   Distribution of Personality Types**

| Personality Type | General Population Base | Educator Base | Educator Phase |
|---|---|---|---|
| Feeler | 30% | 41% | 21% |
| Thinker | 25% | 12% | 24% |
| Believer | 10% | 36% | 29% |
| Dreamer | 10% | 4% | 10% |
| Funster | 20% | 7% | 10% |
| Doer | 5% | — | 6% |

base of being *adaptable, persuasive, and charming* and experiencing the world through actions. Also noteworthy were the data indicating that 20 percent of the group was Feeler base/Believer phase and 14 percent of the group was Believer base/Feeler phase. The graphic comparisons are shown in the figures in table B.2.

People whose base and phase are the same have not experienced a need to move above their base characteristics—that is, their perceptions, needs, and other aspects of their personalities are all drawn from their base. The base and phase frequencies are shown in table B.2.

Again, the concept of *phase* is unique to the Process Communication Model and adds to its comprehensiveness. Experiencing a phase change means that one's motivators change. If one is a Feeler (base) in Believer phase, then that person is most easily motivated by *recognition for work* and *acceptance of convictions*—these are the psychological needs of Believers. However, that individual still experiences the world most easily through feelings (Feeler perceptual preferences) but, in this case, will

**Table B.2   Educator Demographics**

| Base | Phase | | | | | | Total |
|---|---|---|---|---|---|---|---|
| | Feeler | Thinker | Believer | Dreamer | Funster | Doer | |
| Feeler | 4 | 23 | 48 | 13 | 9 | 2 | 99 |
| Thinker | 7 | — | 13 | 2 | 2 | 5 | 29 |
| Believer | 34 | 32 | 3 | 5 | 10 | 3 | 87 |
| Dreamer | 2 | — | 4 | 4 | — | — | 10 |
| Funster | 4 | 3 | 3 | 1 | 3 | 3 | 17 |
| Doer | — | — | — | — | — | — | — |
| Total | 51 | 58 | 71 | 25 | 24 | 13 | 242 |

appear more like a Believer, in many of the words, tones, dress, and environmental preferences of the Believer-type person.

One of the more interesting categories generated from the Kahler (1996) *Personality Pattern Inventory* is interaction span—the amount of relative energy one has to deal with other personality types. Given the distribution arrayed above, it is not surprising that most educators interact most easily (with the most available energy) with others like themselves. The data also showed a comparatively low amount of energy of educators in interacting with those most dissimilar to themselves. Table B.3 shows the interaction span of the sample. (Note: The numbers reflect the relative amount of energy as a percentage. For example, these educators had the ability to interact with Feelers with relative ease because, as a group, they had 69 percent of the available Feeler "energy.")

Educators in the sample had high levels of energy to interact with Feelers, Thinkers, and Believers. They also had a commensurately low amount of energy to interact with Dreamers, Funsters, and Doers. What this means in practical terms is that those students who are most like them will thrive, and those least like them will flounder. This echoes the student performance information reported by Gilbert (1994) above.

## Results

The overall mean of the 322 people who completed the Watson-Barker Listening Test (WBLT) was 15.30 out of a possible 20. This converts to a mean score of 76.5, more than 15 percent above the national median of 66 and the national mean of 66.4, both normed on a pretest basis in 1991 with a group of more than 3,700 managers, supervisors, and professionals (Watson and Barker 1995). The five subscores on the

**Table B.3    Interaction Span of Educators**

|          |    |
|----------|----|
| Feeler   | 69 |
| Thinker  | 69 |
| Believer | 72 |
| Dreamer  | 32 |
| Funster  | 36 |
| Doer     | 25 |

WBLT are: (1) evaluating message content (CONTENT), (2) understanding meaning in conversations (CONVERS), (3) understanding and remembering information (REMEMB), (4) evaluating emotional meanings in messages (EVALEMO), and (5) following directions and instructions (DIRECTNS).

The WBLT-short version contains twenty questions. The scores on each four-response subtest were multiplied by 5 to convert it to a possible total of 100, the basis on which the national norms were calculated for the longer version. The means for each of the subscores, raw and converted, are shown in table B.4.

The lowest subscore for the sample group of educators was in *following directions and instructions,* 12.5 percent below the national norm. All of the other subscores exceeded national norms by 10 to 60 percent, with *understanding meaning in conversations* showing the highest difference. The area of greatest proficiency was *evaluating emotional meanings in messages,* exceeding the national norm by 14 percent.

When comparing the mean subscores with each other using multiple t-tests, some significant differences were noted. They appear on the matrix shown in table B.5. These data indicated that the weakest area of response—*following directions and instructions*—was significantly lower than three of the four other subscores; the strongest area—*evaluating emotional responses in messages*—was significantly higher than any of the other subscores.

Using analyses of variance, no significant differences were found when examining the overall WBLT score with each of the independent variables. That is, regardless of gender, work level, or sector, the sample of educators listened with equal effectiveness. Additionally, no differ-

**Table B.4  Watson-Barker Listening Test Scores**

|  | Raw | Converted | Norm | Percent Diff. |
|---|---|---|---|---|
| CONTENT | 3.19 | 15.95 | 12.8 | +24.6 |
| CONVERS | 2.83 | 14.15 | 8.8 | +60.8 |
| REMEMB | 3.15 | 15.75 | 14.2 | +10.9 |
| EVALEMO | 3.33 | 16.65 | 14.6 | +14.0 |
| DIRECTNS | 2.80 | 14.00 | 16.0 | −12.5 |
| Total | 15.3 | 76.50 | 66.4 | +15.2 |

Table B.5    **Watson-Barker Listening Test, Subscore Comparison Significance**

|          | CONTENT | CONVERS | REMEMB | EVALEMO | DIRECTNS |
|----------|---------|---------|--------|---------|----------|
| CONTENT  |         | ***     |        | *       | ***      |
| CONVERS  | ***     |         | ***    | ***     |          |
| REMEMB   |         | ***     |        | **      | ***      |
| EVALEMO  | *       | ***     | **     |         | ***      |
| DIRECTNS | ***     |         | ***    | ***     |          |

Note: The differences between the means were significant: $^{\circ}p < .05$; $^{\circ\circ}p < .01$; $^{\circ\circ\circ}p < .001$.

ences were found in listening effectiveness between collegiate and pre-collegiate educators when they were regrouped in that fashion.

The PCM variables were the main focus of the research. No differences were found in the listening effectiveness of the sample on the overall WBLT score or any of the subscores when using base and phase designations.

Each completed PPI revealed whether or not the responses had *Questionable Validity* (QV). This is a category that reveals if a respondent: (a) consciously or unconsciously wants the results to appear favorable, (b) perceives the inventory as a test, or (c) is experiencing some physical or emotional distress. The sample was divided into two groups—those with and those without QV. No differences in performance on the WBLT were found.

## Discussion

It was anticipated (presumed) that educators who are more intrinsically motivated and withdrawn (Thinkers and Believers) would listen more effectively than any of the other personality types because they preferred auditory input. This was not the case with the representative sample of educators from both the collegiate and precollegiate arenas; no significant differences were found. Further, the group mean on the overall score on the Watson-Barker Listening Test was 15 percent higher than an extrapolated national norm.

Prior to the data collection, the presumption of difference was based on the various orientations and descriptions of the personality types identified by the Process Communication Model (Kahler 1982). Thinkers and Believers are motivated by recognition for work—a focus on accomplishment acknowledged by others and a certain precision in functioning. They experience the world through *thoughts* and *opinions,* respectively. Knowing that Feelers are more people-oriented and need acceptance of self, that Dreamers prefer solitude with little or no interaction with others, and that Funsters and Doers need the more kinesthetic interaction of playful contact and incidence led the researcher to the construct that there would be a difference in listening performance.

The lack of significant difference in performance raises the question of whether educators are unique in several ways. This uniqueness might project to the achievement orientation most educators would have— predominantly for their students or colleagues and, by example or extension, for themselves. That is, regardless of any extant preference or need, when called upon to perform, educators can do so. Achieving well on a listening test, especially a short one, might have been perceived as a challenge and an attainable one. Hence, these data suggested a distinction to be made between *performance* and *preference*—but the research design did not allow for this distinction to be verified.

The researcher, who oversaw the administration of all of the listening tests, observed some consistent flagging of attention as the test progressed. This may account for the poorer scores in *following instructions and directions,* which was the last subtest. Villaume and Weaver (1996) echoed that the longer version of the WBLT might also be fatiguing.

The ancillary outcomes were more interesting—those that related to the personality distribution of the sample of educators and the marked differences in the potential to interact with other personality types. Educators, as represented by the sample, predominate with three personalities—Feelers, Thinkers, and Believers. They were either based (89 percent) or phased (74 percent) with one of the types, or combined (68 percent) in base and phase with two of the three predominant types. Equally interesting was that there were no base Doers, and base Funsters were only 10 percent of the sample (as opposed to the 20 percent North American distribution); 16 percent of the group were phase Funsters or Doers.

This sample of educators, attributable to their personality-type distribution, had ample energy to interact with Feelers, Thinkers, and Believers. Conversely, they had very limited energy to interact with Dreamers, Funsters, and Doers.

### Summary and Implications

Gilbert (1988, 1989) reported that listening is required in classrooms and in other educational situations a majority of the time, but most educators have had little or no formal training in learning and teaching the *skill* of listening. The result has been that much is lost when auditory input is the sole technique for conveying information (Steil, Barker, and Watson 1983). Since the gap between the need for listening and preparation in listening appeared to be consistent, the researcher wanted to examine whether certain types of educators listened more effectively than others. The representative sample of educators did not demonstrate significant differences in the performance of listening as measured by the Watson-Barker Listening Test.

Because of the researcher's familiarity with the Process Communication Model, which was used to type the subjects in the sample, questions were raised as to whether a short (twenty-minute) test was extensive enough to measure performance when other information about the personality types suggested different preferences in perceptions, needs, and interaction. An article published by Villaume and Weaver (1996) after the current research was completed suggested the WBLT may need to be revamped to be able to distinguish between the various submeasures by varying the degree of difficulty of the items. If the WBLT were to be revised, it might produce enough variability to allow any significant differences to surface—or, if available, another measure should be sought that examines the types of listening educators do and expect of their students. Also, an expanded version of the research design might include a brief survey of input preferences—auditory, visual, kinesthetic, or tactile. (Note: The original research was done in 1995. The WBLT has since been revised to a forty-item instrument.)

A more conclusive outcome from the research was verification of predominant educator types and the potential to interact with others. Not surprisingly, educators have the potential to interact most easily with others like themselves. However, the sample demonstrated very limited potential to interact with those unlike themselves—types that comprise 35 percent of the general population, are more extrinsically motivated, and who may respond more preferably to something other than the typical auditory and visual emphases in most classrooms. What this means is that educators should consider the preferences of those unlike themselves and find the *energy* and *strategies* to deal with them effectively, rather than insisting that they adapt to what is most comfortable for educators. Accomplishing this shift in approach requires that educators arrange to get their own needs met and find sufficient energy to deal with others using different perceptions and motivational techniques, especially since many of these *others* might be categorized as at risk.

## REFERENCES

Gilbert, M. B. 1988. Listening in school: I know you can hear me—but are you listening? *Journal of the International Listening Association* 2: 121–32.

———. 1989. Perceptions of listening behaviors of school principals. *School Organisation* 9: 271–82.

———. 1994. Meeting communication needs of students can promote success. Little Rock: University of Arkansas. Unpublished report of Off-campus Duty Assignment.

Kahler, T. 1982. *Process communication model: A contemporary model for organizational development*. Little Rock, Ark.: Kahler Communications.

———. 1996. *Personality pattern inventory*. Little Rock, Ark.: Kahler Communications.

Roberts, C. 1986. A validation of the Watson-Barker listening test. *Communication Research Reports* 3: 115–99.

———. 1988. The validation of listening tests: Cutting the Gordian knot. *Journal of the International Listening Association* 2: 1–19.

Steil, L. K., L. L. Barker, and K. W. Watson. 1983. *Effective listening*. Reading, Mass.: Addison-Wesley.

Villaume, W. A., and J. B. Weaver III. 1996. A factorial approach to establishing reliable listening measures from the WBLT and the KCLT: Full information factor analysis of dichotomous data. *International Journal of Listening* 10: 1–20.

Watson, K. W., and L. L. Barker. 1995. *Watson-Barker listening test*. New Orleans, La.: Spectra (revised video, short form).

# Appendix C

## Student Grades as a Function of Personality Match with Their Teachers: What Happened in Sheridan? (Excerpted from Gilbert 1994)

### WHAT HAPPENED IN SHERIDAN?

In November and December 1992, twenty staff members at Sheridan (Arkansas) High School underwent two days of training on the Kahler Process Teaching Model (KTPM) (Kahler 1995a), the teaching application of Process Communication, facilitated by the author. During the two days, individuals were debriefed on the components of the KTPM, including their own personality profiles (*Key to Me for Educators* [Kahler 1995b]), character strengths of the various personalities, personality structuring, phasing, perception, psychological needs, communication channels, driver behaviors, and failure mechanisms. Suggestions were made as to the classroom/educational aspects of the components.

The author began the 1993–94 academic year as a visiting member of the faculty, with the full approval and accord of the district superintendent and the school principal. He was introduced at the initial faculty meeting, and his purpose for being on campus was explained. That purpose was to observe the interactions of those individuals who had been trained in the KTPM with students and to provide reinforcement/suggestions for other interactional strategies. Additionally, students were to be profiled. Faculty who had not undergone the training were invited

163

to ask the author to visit their classrooms and were also informed that he would be visiting on a random basis.

Seventeen of the twenty educators who had been trained in KTPM concepts were still on staff when the project began. The strongest personality parts of all the trainees are listed in table C.1.

It has been documented that educators are predominantly Believers, Feelers, and Thinkers, beyond the broader distribution patterns cited above. In the case of the Sheridan staff, 90 percent of the staff were either Believer, Feeler, or Thinker in their base or their phase, compared to less than 43 percent for the profiled students.

Students were chosen for profiling because of observed failure patterns (either academically or behaviorally), teacher request, participation in advanced-placement activities, or student request. Some students who were identified because of observed failure patterns did not return the response cards from which profiles could be generated. The responses of six students fell into a pattern that suggested they wanted to be perceived well; six other students responded in a way that suggested they viewed the inventory as a test (Kahler 1982).

Table C.2 shows that the profiled students were 46 percent Funsters and Doers in either their base or their phase, which compares to less than 8 percent of the same types for the staff. What this means is that those students who were at risk would probably be in greater risk when confronted by teachers weak in Funster and Doer energy. This observation is supported by the only statistically significant interaction. An analysis of variance comparing grade point average with interaction energy yielded an F-ratio of 5.16 (total degrees of freedom = 39), which was significant at the .001 level. While these data reinforce conclusions from

**Table C.1 Base and Phase Personality Structure of Faculty, Sheridan High School, 1993**

| Personality Type | Base | Phase |
| --- | --- | --- |
| Dreamer | | 1 |
| Believer | 6 | 8 |
| Doer | | |
| Funster | 1 | 2 |
| Feeler | 9 | 4 |
| Thinker | 4 | 5 |
| Total | 20 | 20 |

**Table C.2    Base and Phase Personality Structure of Students, Sheridan High School, 1993–94**

| Personality Type | Base | Phase |
|------------------|------|-------|
| Dreamer | 6 | 3 |
| Believer | 8 | 4 |
| Doer | 4 | 8 |
| Funster | 12 | 14 |
| Feeler | 10 | 8 |
| Thinker | 1 | 4 |
| Total | 41 | 41 |

other previous studies, caution should be exercised because of the limited number of subjects.

When student grade point average was compared with the ability to interact with each of the personality types, the correlations were the weakest in interactions with Funsters and Doers; the correlations were strongest in interactions with Feelers, Thinkers, Believers, and Dreamers. Table C.3 shows the correlations.

What these data suggest is that students with higher GPAs can interact with the personality types most like their teachers better than those who do not. This supports the notion that grades are partially the ability of students to meet teacher expectations. With Doers and Funsters having Thinker as one of the weaker parts of their personality structure, this finding is not surprising.

When student profiles were generated, a debriefing occurred with the student to explain the profile and its use. A copy of the profile was given to the student and another copy, with a parent/guardian permission slip attached, was placed in the student's permanent record folder.

**Table C.3    Correlations of Interaction Energy with Student Grade Point Average, Sheridan High School, 1994**

| Personality Type | |
|------------------|--------|
| Dreamer | 0.3396 |
| Believer | 0.3591 |
| Doer | −0.2496 |
| Funster | 0.0889 |
| Feeler | 0.4101 |
| Thinker | 0.3660 |

Being an on-site consultant was quite helpful to the staff. For example, one youngster (who did not return a response card) was identified early as in some distress by both the teacher and me. I suggested to the teacher that he be more playful in his interactions with the student as a means of energizing him. (The teacher was a base Feeler in a Thinker phase and had Funster as last in his personality structure.) Recent standardized test scores had shown this student to be on a downward slide and his current standing was in the lower third of his class with regard to grade point average. He passed the state minimum performance test at the eighth grade by a ten-point margin of a possible 4,200 points. He had a low C/high D in the teacher's class, a major accomplishment for the student. The teacher reported him to be a willing and active participant in class, attributable in part to the teacher's attempt to meet the student's needs positively by playing with him, supporting the students' effort, and encouraging greater self-esteem. Other measures of the student's progress are a pronounced willingness to establish eye contact with the teacher and more erect posture. (The teacher was able to do this because of having his own needs met and sufficient energy to move into the student's frame of preference.)

The major drawback to the findings is that only a small group of students were profiled. Many of the students who demonstrated distress patterns were unwilling to complete the inventories, even with repeated requests by the author and attempts to support the requests by the principal. Many of the cells in the various data analyses simply had too few numbers to allow meaningful outcomes to be produced.

## REFERENCES

Gilbert, M. B. 1994. Meeting communication needs of students can promote success. Little Rock: University of Arkansas. Unpublished report of Off-Campus Duty Assignment.

Kahler, T. 1982. *The process communication management seminar.* Little Rock, Ark.: Kahler Communications.

———. 1995a. *The process teaching model seminar.* Little Rock, Ark.: Kahler Communications.

———. 1995b. *Key to me for educators profile.* Little Rock, Ark.: Kahler Communications.

# Appendix D

## Dealing with Distress: Suggestions for Responses to Behaviors

This material has been adapted with permission from T. Kahler, *The advanced process communication seminar* (Little Rock, Ark.: Kahler Communications, 1996) and T. Kahler, *Key to me for students profile* (Little Rock, Ark.: Kahler Communications, 1996).

### DEALING WITH DISTRESS

#### Withdraws

This is the second-degree distress you will see from someone in Dreamer phase, being driven by "I have to be strong to be OK." Most likely she is not getting her *solitude* need met. An initial response might be, "Dorothy, you have been asked to do a lot of things. Take this afternoon off and do something for yourself."

Other things you can do:

- Give her clear directions, then leave her alone
- Give her an office/work place out of the mainstream
- Assign her data collecting/doing "quiet" research (library, etc.)
- Establish routines for her to do repetitive tasks

#### Overcontrols

This is the second-degree distress you will see from someone in Thinker phase, being driven by "I have to be perfect to be OK." Most likely he is not getting his *recognition for work* or *time structure* needs met. An initial response might be, "Alfred, you do good work. How long do you think it will take you to come up with options to deal with the problem we are facing? What do you see the alternatives to be?"

Other things you can do:

- Set priorities for projects
- Focus on doing what is most important
- Arrange for acknowledgment of his accomplishments
- Set clear times frames and responsibilities
- Assign him tasks with tangible outcomes of completion
- Invite him to attending workshops to increase his skills or expertise/data base

### Becomes Vindictive

This is the second-degree distress you will see from someone in Doer phase, being driven by "you have to be strong to be OK." Most likely he is not getting his *incidence* need met. An initial response might be, "Doug, tell me what you see the bottom line to be and how long it will take to get there." (Again, it is unlikely you will see many people with strong Doer energy in education. They will choose other avenues or set themselves up to be eliminated.)

Other things you can do:

- Involve him in projects/tasks with quick rewards/payoffs
- Allow him to compete positively with co-workers
- Involve him in physical/kinesthetic things
- Direct him to get to the "bottom line" as quickly as he needs
- Involve him in exciting projects
- Let him understand the "perks" for assigned tasks well before deadlines
- When appropriate, have him travel on professional business as often as possible

### Preaches

This is the second-degree distress you will see from someone in Believer phase, being driven by "you have to be perfect to be OK." Most likely he is not getting his *recognition for work* or *conviction* needs met. An initial response might be, "Matthew, you are an important member of our staff. Your contributions are valuable. Your perspective contributes to our seeing a full picture of our direction."

Other things you might do:

- Share your personal values and beliefs
- Ask him to establish rules, structure, or procedures for projects
- Assign him the proposing/implementing projects that affirm his belief system
- Ask him to mentor a colleague or less experienced person

### Blames

This is the second-degree distress you will see from someone in Funster phase, being driven by "I have to be try hard to be OK." Most likely she is not getting her *playful contact* needs met. An initial response might be, "Angie, I like the great enthusiasm and fresh approaches you bring to our staff. Wow! I am glad we have your energy to help us."

Other things you might do:

- Joke with her
- Tell her jokes and amusing anecdotes
- Use word play and puns with her
- Allow her to play *before* working

### Invites Criticism

This is the second-degree distress you will see from someone in Feeler phase, being driven by "I have to please you to be OK." Most likely she is not getting her *acceptance of self* or *sensory* needs met. An initial response might be, "Barbara, you are so caring. The warmth you bring to our staff allows us to be comfortable in difficult situations—and even when things are not difficult. Thank you."

Other things you might do:

- Allow her to create her own "nest" at work
- Arrange to recognize and accept her as a person
- Assign her to lead and work with groups of people who appreciate her
- Assign her to work on projects that help others

# About the Author

**Michael Gilbert** is professor of educational leadership at Central Michigan University. He has been involved in the preparation of educational leaders since 1975. His earlier career involved public school teaching and administration at both the school site and central office.